**ALSO BY ERICA WERNICK**

*LA Bound: The Ultimate Guide To Moving To Los Angeles*

# Meant for This

THE MINDSET AND STRATEGY
TO ACHIEVE YOUR MOST
"IMPOSSIBLE" DREAMS

ERICA WERNICK

ISBN: 978-1-09835-116-8 (paperback)

For Mom, Dad, and Meryl, who have
supported every dream I've felt meant for.

# Praise

*So real. So relatable. So refreshing.*

**ROSS CHISARI**

*It is now 1:15am and I can't put the book down even though I usually go to bed at 10. Content is extraordinary, voice is unique, and the system is easy to follow. Would reread 100 times and recommend to everyone!*

**MALAK DABCHA**

*I have been a successful, working cinematographer for 30 years. Even with all my years of experience, Erica astounds me with novel insights, fresh, actionable strategies and fierce inspiration to level up my career.*

*I mentor young and aspiring filmmakers. As I read the book I was continually excited to share these words with each of them, so much so that on several occasions I snapped and texted photos of specific paragraphs which spoke directly to a particular individual's questions, concerns or challenges.*

*This is the very best, most honest, and affirming coaching I have ever experienced for this notoriously tricky industry. To quote Erica herself, reading this book is like "taking an Opportunity cake out of the oven."*

**BRAD RUSHING**

*Erica, as a teacher, has such exciting and motivating energy and I think that's what makes this book stand out. It makes the artist feel like they are a star already. I would recommend this book to EVERY actor!*

**AMANDA KRUGER**

*This book is amazing and addicting and exactly what this industry needs.*

**KARLA OJEDA**

*As someone who has worn many hats in this business, I can tell you first hand that having a game plan in this town is essential. In "Meant for This," this witty, honest, and vulnerable look behind the curtain of tinseltown, gives you just that: a blueprint for success, a strategy for following your dreams and the mindset needed to be fearless in the pursuit of them. "Meant For This" is the perfect balance between self-help book and good storytelling. My only regret is this book was not around 15 years ago when I was starting out on my own journey.*

MARK HAAPALA

*I just finished this book and I'm literally in tears because it's so beautiful and positive and inspiring. Erica's genuine positivity is truly astounding. I've never read a book like it before.*

EMMY NEWMAN

*Erica's book takes away the mystique of Hollywood. Her strategies, how to inhabit your next level before you get there and her own personal rise shows artists anything is possible. This book will change your life.*

AMY SHAFFNER

*It's so good! I genuinely wish I had a book like this in college. It would have saved me so much heartache (and time, probably).*

CHELSEY MARCH

*"Meant for This" speaks to the star inside of you and awakens the dreams you've kept on the back burner for far too long. This book makes you an instant Hollywood insider, who not only knows the secrets to making your dreams come true, but understands the common blocks that stand in the way and how to overcome them immediately. If you're ready for a book that goes beyond self help cliches and gives you a practical path directly to the red carpet, get this book and get ready to take notes, because your career is about to change. There's nowhere you can't go using the inspiration, principles, and practices taught by Erica!*

STEPHEN LOVEGROVE

# Contents

*Meant for This*

*Being realistic is the most commonly
traveled road to mediocrity.*
**WILL SMITH**

# *Introduction*

There is no dream too big or too impossible. Whatever it is that's calling you, you can have. The problem is that not enough people are telling you that. In fact, most people are telling you the opposite. And they've told you this for so long, that you've likely bought into it and repeat it to yourself.

After spending a decade in Hollywood, the industry notorious for big dreams, I've heard every discouraging belief under the sun: "You want to succeed in Hollywood? That's like winning the lottery. Good luck!" (The most sarcastic "good luck" you've ever heard.) "You're going to be waiting tables your whole life." ("Starving artists" are, after all, two words that are rarely seen without each other.) "That's going to be really hard." "It's rare that you'll make it." Blah, blah, scarcity. Blah, blah, fail, fail, fail.

This narrative is so deeply ingrained that you hear it from books, from mentors, from teachers, from peers, even family members. One time, I read a chapter or so of a book for actors, written by a famous actor, and I basically had a temper tantrum and dramatically tossed it to the floor after reading discouraging statement after discouraging statement. I know, totally mature and easy-breezy cool. But the feeling was mutual amongst my clients, and that brings me to today: **I've had enough of this limiting bullshit.**

Here's the thing—I know our biggest dreams are going to come with some challenges. They are big dreams for a reason, and every big accomplishment comes with its own set of obstacles. But you, you fancy dreamer, need to hear something beyond, "This is going to be hard." Because, chances are, if you're anything like me, that "hard" nonsense isn't going to stop you from pursuing your dreams. It might rattle you a little. It might make you second guess, and ponder pursuing something more "realistic." But that dream you feel meant for will not go away. That dream will never shut up. It will whisper, it will scream, it will shake you—whatever it needs to do to get your attention and tell you that you must pursue this. So if you *must* pursue this, wouldn't it be great to finally talk to someone and say, "Cool, it's going to be hard. I'm up for it. Now what?" The conversation must continue. That's what this book is for. I see you. I see your dream. I'm honored to hold space for it and let it flourish. I'm here to inspire you, cheer you on, and show you how to make your "impossible" dreams totally possible.

I'll be the first to admit that I have a bit of a fairy-tale idea of dreams. But that's never been a hindrance for me...in fact, it's been the key to my success. It's how I keep going when the obstacles show up, or when I feel impatient. It's why I go for it in the first place. And it's led to over 60 television shows and films for myself and my clients on Netflix,

Hulu, HBO, and every other major network (even in the "hardest" industry). My belief in what's possible, and the positive narrative I've cultivated, has literally led to countless artists achieving their dreams through the systems I've developed. So, the naysayers can suck it! We can totally live in a fairy tale world where our dreams come true, and I have the proof to back it up.

In this book, you're going to learn everything you need to succeed at your biggest dreams. I walk you through a step-by-step process, with tangible actions you can take **today**. This book will inspire you to believe in yourself like you've never believed before. Whether you dream of being on Broadway, winning an Emmy, starting your own business, or making millions of dollars, your "impossible" dream is just a few chapters away.

Twelve years ago, I had a dream in my heart to design graphics for television. That dream kept calling me, and it led me to Los Angeles. I was from a suburb outside of Philadelphia, so 3,000 miles away from LA, and I didn't know a single person in the industry. Hollywood is so much about who you know, and I knew no one. No uncle's best friend's neighbor, no high school friend's parent, no hair stylist's cousin. I was alone. But I didn't let that stop me and I freaking broke in, anyway. Within two weeks of moving to Los Angeles, I booked my first TV show. So I know what it's like to want something so badly that it hurts when you don't have it. And I also know what it's like to finally get the dream. The latter feeling is so indescribably fulfilling that I want you to feel it, too. That's why you need to read this book.

If I were your dream, you know what I'd say to you?

I'd say, "Thank you. Thank you for not giving up on me. I'm still here and I know we can do this."

You *can* do this.

The systems in this book have worked for actors, writers, directors, VFX editors, singers, makeup artists, high school teachers, entrepreneurs, talk show hosts, producers, music supervisors, artists, production assistants, psychologists, and even a retired U.S. Patent Commissioner. It will work for you, too, as soon as you begin to implement.

You deserve all your dreams. I don't care how big or impossible others deem them.

Read this book. Prove them wrong. And live the life you've always dreamed of.

**PART 1**

# Think Like A Star

*You don't attract what you want.*
*You attract what you are.*

**WAYNE DYER**

# *One*

# MAKING THE "IMPOSSIBLE" POSSIBLE: THE BLUEPRINT

The list had been posted. I frantically scanned it, searching for my name. I desperately wanted to see it on there, I needed to see it on there. If my name wasn't on that list, I didn't know what I was going to do with my life. My dreams would be crushed before they even began. The list wasn't long, there were only 20 names, so it only took a moment to discover...

"OH MY GOD!! I GOT IN!!!"

There was my name, "Erica Wernick," on the list of students who had been selected for the Graphic Design major. The list that says only 20 out of the 45 of us were moving on to pursue graphic design in college. My dreams were officially beginning.

See, the design school I was trying to get into didn't open up the major until junior year. That meant I spent my first two years of college not even knowing if I'd be able to study the thing I wanted to study. I had to take prerequisites and put a portfolio together, and then, maybe, I could pursue this major halfway through my college experience.

Even though I had never taken design classes before, I still knew this was my calling. It was confirmed one day when I spoke to a friend who was a year ahead of me.

"How's the program? Do you love it?" I excitedly asked. I was hoping to get a glimpse into my dreamy future.

"Eh, it's OK. I'm taking this class that's all about fonts. It's so boring," my friend replied. To a normal person, this would totally burst their fantasy bubble, but for me, it did the opposite.

"An entire class about fonts? THAT SOUNDS AWESOME!"

A design nerd was born. And that's when I knew this dream in my heart was a true one.

When I finally made it to my first official class, I couldn't have been more of a cliché: sitting at the table closest to the professor, eager as hell to learn everything about graphic design. It was my own little Rachel Berry moment. I was here to succeed and live my dreams, and no one could get in my way!

Our first assignment was a crazy project for a first time graphic design student: we had to combine photography with typography (fonts, essentially, my favorite thing in the world—oh my gosh, please still like me, I swear I can be cool.). I put so much energy and work into this assignment. To quote Morales from *A Chorus Line* (and give a little foreshadowing), "I dug right down to the bottom of my soul and I tried."

The day we got our grades back, I was floating on top of the world. Not only did I receive an "A" but the professor held my project up in front of the class as an example of a great design! I mean, holy crap. Could it be any clearer that I'm on the right track? This validation solidified it for me.

Then came the second assignment. I channeled my inner High Achiever and got to work. The same enthusiasm carried me through, my work ethic never dipping below excellent. When you find something that feels like your calling, and you really care, you go all in. That's what I was doing. No half-assing for me.

The fateful day came where we received our grades for this second project. When I got mine, I couldn't believe what I saw. It was a "D." I had never gotten a D in my life. The computer lab was buzzing with energy and the light from the screens felt bright and cheery. But darkness loomed around me as I felt my own light begin to dim. I sank deep into my chair and felt completely crushed. How did this happen? There were no notes of explanation so I was at a total loss. I had no idea how I went from the star pupil to almost failing. What came next changed my life forever.

As I was sulking, the professor wheeled up next to me in a computer chair. "What happened there, Erica?" She asked. "I guess you just got lucky on that first one."

A proverbial knife stabbed me in the heart. With that one phrase, my dream was destroyed.

I ran to the bathroom and balled my eyes out. I was devastated. Here I was, pursuing my dream, and my professor, the person who is supposed to teach me, said that anything I had done well up to this point was just luck.

As I went through the rest of the semester, I learned that this professor used fear as a teaching tactic. By December, I hadn't really learned anything new about graphic design. But I did learn one thing: that I'm the only one who gets to decide whether or not I can succeed at my dream, and I'm definitely the only one who determines if it's worth pursuing at all. So I packed up my stuff and pulled a Morales—I found another class. The next year I transferred schools and finally learned how to be a good designer.

My dream was destroyed in a moment, but that moment was exactly that—a *moment*. I reconnected with my belief in myself. I reconnected with my dream. And I decided it was still going to happen. After graduating from my new university, I moved to Los Angeles and broke into Hollywood. Over the past 12 years, I've designed graphics for over 30 television shows and films. And not a single second of it was due to luck.

The attainability of our dreams is a decision within us. It begins with a belief and that's the seed we plant. Greatness is more accessible than we think...as long as we can hold the vision through any obstacle thrown our way.

Even now, when I have a new dream, the doubts still come rushing to the surface. Who am I to achieve this? I'm not special enough. I'm not lovable enough. I'm not talented enough. It sounds like my voice, but those doubts are inevitably built by ghosts of failures past. It makes the dream feel outside of me, like this unreachable thing that's cute in theory, but ultimately destined for someone else. Those old stories combined with the "bigness" of the dream builds a strong case for it being impossible. But I know that greatness is accessible for *all of us*. Abraham Hicks has said the first mistake we make in this process is calling it a "big" dream. Abraham says as long as we use the word "big" to describe it, we keep it out of reach. We can make it accessible simply by changing the label. It's just a dream. Not *big*. Just a dream.

What's crazy is that since I've accomplished my Hollywood dream, and lived it for over a decade, it doesn't feel "big" to me. Someone looking in from the outside (like my friends and family back home) would certainly call it a big dream. But since I've accomplished it, it doesn't feel big. It feels right here, in the palm of my hand. And in comparison to other people's accomplishments, it feels small.

So, I know. I know that the dreams within you are reachable. I know that greatness is attainable. The "Oh my gosh but HOW will I ever make this happen?" and the voice inside your head that questions your worthiness and deservedness, makes these dreams feel completely "big" and out of reach. But that's all an illusion. The wall we put up between ourselves and our dreams is built by us. We chose to put it up there and we can choose to take it down.

When I first began my Hollywood journey, I had a very supportive cousin who recommended I read a book called *The Success Principles* by Jack Canfield. In that book, I read a line that changed my life: "It has been estimated that someone in America becomes a millionaire every

4 minutes." This blew my mind. I grew up believing that millionaires were rare and that only special people become millionaires. I mean, every 4 minutes? That means it's normal, it's achievable. This was my first experience with reeling a dream in—taking away the "big" element, and making it attainable. Some call this "normalizing," where you literally make your big dream seem normal.

Ever since then, I've had this ability to dream bigger than anyone I know, and truly believe in that dream's possibility. It's almost become a superpower. But I don't want to keep it for myself. I want you to have it, too. I want my belief to become contagious. That's why I'm writing this book and what this chapter is all about. I've connected to this as my purpose in life, to share the message that **any dream is possible.**

If you've been brave enough to declare a big dream of yours, I know you may have been met with disbelief (from others and even yourself). People love to tell you how hard this will be and how rare it is to succeed. While data may prove those statements to be true, I've come to realize that data is only true for the people who believe it.

I think any dream is going to have challenges; whether you're trying to win an Oscar or start your own business. The challenges are part of our journey and contribute to our character and the lessons we must learn. The challenges make the destination oh-so-much sweeter. The idea that your dream pursuit will have challenges, is a given. But the "rare" part, the concept that says, "this isn't possible for you," is a belief you don't have to take on. It doesn't have to be part of your story. It certainly wasn't part of mine.

After a decade in Hollywood, here's what I've learned: There will always be two pools. The first pool is a large group of people who are struggling in their dream pursuit. They struggle to get opportunities, they struggle financially, they struggle mentally. They also see their struggle as a badge of honor, and they'll fight for that honor to prove they have it the hardest. We'll call this pool, "Most People." The second pool is a smaller group of people who are living their dream everyday. They are landing opportunities, making lots of money, and feeling fulfilled. We'll call this pool, "High Achievers." Both sets of data are true.

Here's the most important piece that I want you to pay attention to: just because the first pool is bigger, doesn't make it more worthy of your focus. In fact, if you dream of swimming with the High Achievers, it's imperative that you don't focus on the bigger pool of Most People. It's a matter of life and death of your dream. You can swim in the second pool. You don't need to accept the first one as your fate just because it's what everybody else does. If you want to succeed, you can't be like most people. Most people are problem-oriented, focused on scarcity, and repeat limitations that others around them buy into. When you follow the herd, you get the same results as the herd. Instead, you need to be YOU—the most badass version of yourself that's ever lived. (Something you are totally capable of.) High Achievers think and do things differently than Most People (that's why they're successful). Dive into that smaller pool and silence all the other noise. Your dream, whatever it is, is possible. If you believed me, what would you dream?

You can't have a blueprint without knowing what you're building. So many people never make the blueprint because they don't believe it's possible. They buy into the limitations that are consistently preached, and they stay small. They never let themselves dream beyond what they think is possible. Is that you? Have you held yourself back? Have you quieted your dreams because they feel too big?

Sometimes the answer isn't as obvious. Sometimes it's a little more nuanced. At one of my live events, a volunteer came up to the stage for a "Hot Seat." I asked her what her dream was, and she went on and on about acting in movies and television, particularly musical projects where she could sing and dance on screen. This amazing girl lit up and was beaming ear to ear as she described it. "Great!" I told her. "I love this dream! It clearly makes you happy, so let's make it happen!" I prompted her with a strategic question, "What's your first step? What action should you take?"

She paused for a long time. I could see the shift happen: she went from excited energy to completely defeated. The light in her eyes dimmed. Finally, a response:

"I should get a commercial agent and start going out for commercials."

Say whaaaa?! If you don't know anything about Hollywood, let me explain: She didn't say, "Since my dream is to act in TV, I should get a TV agent and start going out for TV shows." She didn't say, "Since my dream is to sing and dance, I should find musicals around LA that I can audition for." Instead, she chose an action that is near-ish to her dream, but far enough to feel within reach. Commercials are like another world, and in Hollywood it's seen as an "easier" world. So it makes perfect sense, that as this girl's belief dwindled she reached for what seemed easier.

When you don't believe your dream is possible, you go for the low hanging fruit—the thing that seems the easiest and is often dream-adjacent. So I asked her, "Why should you be doing commercials? How will that lead to you singing in a TV show or movie?" (To give more information, acting in a commercial rarely leads to acting in a TV show because it's a completely different set of contacts and gate keepers with no crossover. Also, in commercials, you're often playing yourself instead of a character, so it's not even acting you would use for a demo reel.)

Her answer was standard, "Well that's what I thought I was supposed to do."

This is a common block to building a dream blueprint. Not only are people afraid to go directly for what they want, but they also do what they think they're "supposed" to do. What they aren't seeing behind the scenes, is that the people who invented what you're "supposed" to do are the people who are also afraid of going directly for their dream. It's fear/disbelief in disguise. The point I want to emphasize is that in order to make your dream tangible, you have to believe it's possible. The blueprint is born from the belief. The only thing you're *supposed* to do is go after your dream...the actual dream in your heart.

When we were kids we were so good at dreaming. In fact, most of the clients I've worked with say that their Hollywood dream began when they were a child. Whether it was acting out scenes for their families, or simply watching a movie in the theater and feeling a magical connection, our childhood was the perfect place to plant the seeds for our future careers. We were limitless, living in an imagined world of possibilities.

As we got older, the "real world" dimmed that light. We became aware of logistics and reality. We saw the Wizard behind the curtain and stopped believing in Santa Clause. And through this process, our dreams became fantasies, rather than real-life possibilities.

What I've found, though, is that our hearts never forget. Whatever dreams we've had may be quieted but they never go away. We can still connect to our heart any time. If you let it, the soft whisper will get louder and louder. Some of us will choose not to listen. The rest of us will eventually answer the call.

So here we are. This is where it begins. In order for me to tell you how to achieve your big dream, you need to first admit that you want this big dream. You need to know where you're going. And my absolute favorite part of all of this, is holding the space for you to dream, without judgement. Whenever I ask my clients what they dream of creating for themselves, there is hesitation and defensive reactions: some people laugh, some people cry. The overarching theme I see over and over is that people haven't been told that what they want is possible. In fact, they've been told the opposite. When a client tells me they want to win an Oscar, they laugh because they're afraid I'll think their dreams are outrageous and impossible. That's the response they're used to. They laugh as to say, "I know, it's crazy!" When they cry, it's out of shock that someone is allowing them to say these dreams out loud and really, truly, hold the space for them.

But here's the thing: people who perceive your dreams as crazy are not **visionaries**. The visionaries of the world see solutions and creations before there is any physical proof. They see it in their mind, and that's all they need to go on. Martin Luther King Jr. saw equality before it existed. Walt Disney saw a theme park succeeding despite people expressing major doubts and negative reviews. And little old me, a girl from the suburbs of Philly, left everything behind to pursue a Hollywood career without a single connection or understanding of the industry.

The people who doubt your dreams are really expressing doubt in themselves. It's a projection of their own limiting beliefs. They can't see themselves ever succeeding in the way you desire, so they extend their limitations to you. Their doubt has absolutely nothing to do with you and your potential. Jack Canfield says you're not given a dream unless you have the capacity to fulfil it. The dream itself determines your potential, not anyone else's opinion.

A few years ago, a new dream came to me: I want to buy a multi-million dollar house in the Hollywood Hills. At first, it scared me. I had my own doubts. How on earth would I make enough money to afford a house at that price point? But as I spent more time with it and allowed it to grow, I knew in my heart this was something I had to go after. That's when I finally felt ready to tell people. Oh-my-god. What a learning experience. People dumped all of their doubts on me. I'll never forget when a coworker responded with a laughter-filled, "Oh yeah, I want to win the lottery, too!" It crushed me. I felt small and dumb for even wanting this. Very few people took my dream seriously.

But what I learned is that it didn't matter. The only person who needed to take my dream seriously was me. Eventually, I began working towards it. I started going to open houses. Over the past three years, I've been to 150 open houses. I learned about the market. I got crystal clear on what I wanted and what was available. I spoke to realtors and lenders. I found my dream builder. I got to know the neighborhoods inside and out. All of this action built my confidence. Buying this house was no longer a pipe-dream, it became something tangible. And I began to talk about it with **certainty**.

It's remarkable how the responses have changed since then. Now, instead of people laughing at me, they're asking for an invitation to the housewarming party. They're cheering me on and telling me, "I know you'll get that house!" My outer world changed because my inner world changed. I believed in my dream so deeply, that my confidence became contagious.

That's what I want for you. I want you to believe in your dreams so deeply that people eagerly jump on the You-train. Whatever you want, whether it's a dream job, a million dollars, an Oscar, or to start your own business, it's all within reach. But you have to believe it. This is where it begins. If you believe it's far away, it will remain far away. If you believe it's within reach, it will absolutely be within reach. You get to decide.

There is a common attitude in the world that says, "I'll take whatever I can get!" It comes from a good place. It comes from humility and willingness to work hard. But if we dig beneath that surface, we'll see the true foundation for that attitude: we're taught that big success is rare. Scarcity is preached everyday. Therefore, you should be so grateful for any crumbs you're given. Like a hungry dog under the table, you throw yourself at the scraps. But the truth is, you are worthy of a feast. You are worthy of a seat at the table, and that seat is 100% available for you.

**THE DREAM LIST**

When we say, "I'll take whatever I can get!" what we're really saying is, "This is all I believe I can get, so I'll take it." But what if you believed you could get more? What if you believed you could actually get all the things you wanted? I want you to make a list of everything you want. When you make this list, I don't want you to write down what you *think* you can get. I don't want you to limit yourself to things you think are "easier" than what you really want. This list is the no-judgement list. It's a list of the dreams in your heart. Don't worry about logistics (that's what the rest of this book is for!). Don't worry about how it will happen or whether or not it's possible. (Spoiler alert: it's ALL possible.) This is the dream list. It's the blueprint for your success. You want an Oscar? Write it down. You want that dream job? Write it down. You want to change the world? Write it down. Remember, you are a visionary.

Something to note as you come up with this list: all of the goals that we set for ourselves are because we think we'll feel a certain way when we get them. We want the feeling, so we want the goal. For example, many actors say they want to be a "working actor." Why? They want to work consistently. Why do they want to work consistently? Because they'll **feel** secure. They will **feel** joy instead of stress. It all comes down to *feeling*.

I know we're diving in deep here, but it's a worthy conversation, one that I hadn't realized until recently. After studying successful people, and even looking at my own success, I've learned two meaningful lessons:

1) The bar is always moving. We always think that when we reach "there," we'll be happy. But that "there" bar is always moving. The feelings are often temporary, and at the end of the day, happiness and peace come from within, not from anything external. Which leads me to #2:

2) Happiness is more fulfilling than external validation. The external stuff can never truly fill you up. It's not the solution to insecurity or unworthiness. Those come from within, so any goal you set to solve those problems will never solve them permanently.

Take a look at the Oscar, for example. Why does someone want an Oscar? There is external validation in an Oscar. So someone may feel accepted in Hollywood if they win an Oscar. They might feel secure in their talent. And many people believe that an Oscar guarantees consistent work (truthfully, it does not). So that will help them feel financially secure. It may help them feel confident and worthy.

An Oscar (or any award) is an incredible goal to set and I don't fault anyone who has that dream. But as you make your list, I want you to think about what will bring you joy, rather than validation. One of my best experiences working in Hollywood, was on an ABC Family (now Freeform) TV show called *Chasing Life*. ABC Family is not the sexiest network in terms of goals that people aim for. It's not as glamorous as Netflix, or even the regular ABC. But it was the most joy I ever had on a job. The cast and crew were amazing, and we were telling a story that was impacting so many lives. I made relationships that I still keep in touch with, five years later. It was my favorite job because it filled me with joy—something I wasn't even smart enough to chase all those years ago. Now, I've learned that joy will take you so much further than any validation.

As humans, many of us are on a life-long journey of loving ourselves and feeling worthy. It's part of what makes us human, and our vulnerability makes us good creators. Because of this, validation can feel like a warm blanket wrapping around you on a winter's day. It's okay to receive it. It's okay to feel that love. But it's also helpful to fill that love on your own so you don't need the external validation to keep you warm. We have so much power within ourselves. When we cultivate it, our creativity and opportunities grow exponentially. You are amazing. You are loved, you are supported. You deserve your dreams, just because you exist. You are a star and it's time you shine. And your dreams are 100% possible, no matter how crazy they seem.

So, now it's your turn—what do you want? Go make that list and then meet me in Chapter 2.

# Two

# STAR POWER

"I have an interview for a TV show!" I excitedly yelled to my parents over the phone. "I'm meeting these two Prop Masters for break-fast!"

I had only been in LA for two weeks, so it's not surprising that my parents were incredulous. "Hmm, is this a real show? Do you know anything about these people?" Throughout my decade in Hollywood, I've been fortunate to have the most supportive parents in the world. It just took them a little while to get on board. To them, a meeting this quickly seemed too good to be true.

"Mom, Dad, I promise it's real. I'll call you after." I quickly hung up and sat down with my LA cousin as she drew me a map of the streets in Hollywood. This was before Waze (and I have a terrible sense of direction) so I had no idea where Sunset Blvd. was in relation to Santa Monica Blvd. I just knew that those were famous streets, and HOLY CRAP, I WAS GOING TO TAKE THEM TO AN INTERVIEW FOR A REAL TV SHOW!

The morning of the breakfast, I nervously drove over to Hugo's in West Hollywood. Even though I was incredibly green and had no idea what I was doing, my naiveté gave me the confidence I needed. I mean, I had just graduated from a prestigious design school, so how hard could this be?

Tim and Jim sat across from me at a booth. They were kind and affable, nothing like the stereotypes you hear about people in Hollywood. Their rhyming names added to the playfulness and they made me feel at ease. This wasn't your typical interview. Tim and Jim hardly asked me any interview-style questions. They didn't waste any time and jumped right into the project, explaining what was needed.

"This show is about an advertising agency. So one of the first graphics we'll need are business cards for our main characters," they explained. Of all the things a TV Prop Master could ask me to design, I feel like the Universe gave me a wink with that business card. In design school, we made business cards for everything. It was a staple. I totally got this.

"Ok, great! What kind of business is this? Upscale? What's the feel of it?" I asked.

Tim and Jim looked at me with approval. "Great question," Tim replied. Oh my gosh. I impressed them.

It wasn't long before I was on set designing that business card. I walked across the soundstage at The Lot Studios, a small studio in the heart of West Hollywood. A TV show about an advertising agency was like a Graphic Designer's dream—I felt so at home on set amongst the layout tables, cutting boards, and graphic posters. It was a synchronistic transition into my Hollywood career.

Past the fake TV set cubicles, I found myself standing next to Eric McCormack. Will from *Will and Grace* was the lead in our show and I got so nervous every time we spoke that I would ramble on and on and tell him my entire life story. (I drunkenly apologized to him for this at the wrap party, but that's a story for another time.) Eric was the nicest guy, and incredibly supportive. "So are you excited? They're going to do an insert shot of your business card!" He cheered me on, knowing this was my first TV graphic ever. (I had no idea what an "insert shot" was. I learned that it's when the camera does a close up on an object. They were going to film a close-up shot of my business card, so the design would clearly be seen by anyone watching.)

It was there, in that moment, that I felt I had made it. Three weeks earlier, I was just a girl in the suburbs of Philly, excited and terrified to move to Los Angeles. And now, I was standing on the set of a real TV show, watching as a famous actor held my design in front of the camera. Like, what is my life?! I had dreamed of this moment and it turned out to be so much better than I could have imagined.

That TV show was the first of many—39 to be exact (at the time of writing this book). And the only way any of it happened, was because I chose to be the successful person I wanted to be before a single credit was on my resume. I embraced my Star Power—the highest version of myself, ready to match my potential. This was something I leaned into early on, and I still use to this day any time I have a new goal. I think it's one of the most important strategies on the journey to pursuing a big dream, and it's not spoken about enough. I feel like I'm about to share a juicy secret with you, but please don't keep it to yourself. Tell everyone! The more people who know how to pursue their dreams and succeed, the more joy we'll have in this world.

Your Star Power has nothing to do with being a performer, other than the nice visual metaphor it provides. There is a line in the movie *The Holiday* that I'm obsessed with. Arthur, the wise, grandfather-like neighbor, says to Iris: "Iris, in the movies we have leading ladies and we have the best friend. You, I can tell, are a leading lady, but for some reason you're acting like the best friend." Iris' reply is gold, please memorize it: "You're so right. You're supposed to be the leading lady of your own life, for God's sake!" I'm smiling even as I type this. I loooooooove that line. This is Star Power. It's realizing that you are the leading person in your own life. It's choosing to be that leading person by feeling worthy of it and accepting it as truth. So many people are walking around acting like the "best friend," never feeling worthy of the leading role. But you have to be your own Star before any external validation gives you that label, in order to succeed in a big way. It has nothing to do with being the center of attention, but simply *owning your greatness.* That greatness exists within you, right now, at this very moment, even without any experience.

Most of us grow up believing that we're not great until we have some proof that shows we are. This concept is called Have-Do-Be, meaning, once I *have* the job, then I'll finally feel confident enough to take the risks, and then I'll *be* happy and successful. We wait for the external thing to make us happy. We wait for the external thing to determine our readiness to believe in ourselves. Whether it's money, a job, a relationship, or any other material item, we think that once we have it then we'll be happy. For example, once I win the gold medal in gymnastics, then I'll finally feel like I'm great at gymnastics.

Makes sense, right? Except true success doesn't work that way. In order to be successful, you need to be the person who would *become* successful. You need to flip it around to Be-Do-Have. If you're going to win the gold medal in gymnastics, you have to be the person who would win that medal. Think about Steven Spielberg. Who was Steven Spielberg before he directed a single film? He was Steven F*$king Spielberg. Before Spielberg was a name people knew, he was given a temporary pass to get onto the Universal Studios lot for a few days to talk to Chuck Silvers, head of the editorial department. Chuck was not able to get a permanent pass for Spielberg, so Spielberg had to find his own way to get on the lot after those few days were up. He decided to show up in a suit, carrying a briefcase, and wave to the guard at the gate, giving the illusion that he worked there. The guard let him in without seeing any badge or pass. This creative risk got Spielberg on the lot anytime he wanted.

Spielberg didn't wait until he had *Jaws* on his resume to be that bold. He didn't wait until he was known as one of the greatest directors in Hollywood history to take risks and put himself out there. Spielberg did those things *first*. He was **being** the person he needed to be in order to create opportunity and gain the success he wanted. *That's* Star Power.

You need to BE the person you want to be before HAVING any recognition. You need to show up as the star you want to be, now. Who was Taylor Swift before she was Taylor Swift? How about Bill Gates? Or JLO? All of these people started with nothing. They all started with zero jobs, zero success. Their success was born from how they decided to show up in the beginning.

## CREATE YOUR OWN REALITY

We get to create the reality we want to have. This is one of the most powerful statements you'll ever hear, so let me say that again: *We get to create the reality we want to have.* Dr. Joe Dispenza explains that most of us believe life is cause and effect, where our external environment causes us to think and feel a certain way (essentially, Have-Do-Be). But we don't have to live this way and be a victim to our external environment. We can actually *cause* an effect by changing our thoughts and feelings *first*, regardless of what's happening outside of us, and watch the external environment change because of it.[1]

What this means, is that if we can feel successful now, and connect to the thoughts and feelings of that successful version of ourselves before any success has physically happened, we can energetically change the quantum field around us, creating new possibilities. We are causing the effect.

Say whaaaa? If you're anything like me and are more of an art brain, that may sound like a bunch of scientific mumbo-jumbo. So here's another visual explanation, often used by Bob Proctor, that explains this well:

Imagine radio frequencies. You're in your car, changing the radio station. There are a few options: you've got AM, and you've got FM. (And if you're really fancy, you've got Satellite.)

Let's say you're listening to AM radio. It's a bunch of talk, talk, talk, and you're feeling ready for some music. You change the station a million times, but you're not having any luck: all that plays is talk radio.

WTF?!

Ah, yes, young grasshopper, you're so smart. In order to hear music, you need to change the *frequency*. Not just the station. Hop up there to FM and dance it out, baby. Once you change to FM, then you can change the station all you want, and you'll get music.

It's the same thing with your thoughts and feelings. Your thoughts and feelings are the frequencies (AM and FM). The actions you take are like changing the station, and the results you get are the station you land on. If you want a different result in your career (or life), you have to change your thoughts and feelings. Just like the radio frequency you're on controls whether you hear talk or music, your thoughts and feelings control the actions you take, which, in turn, control the results you get. Let's break this down into a specific example: Let's say you feel sad and rejected. From that place, you have a thought, "I should go get drunk with my friends." Then you take an action: you call up your friends and get wasted. When you're good and drunk and drowning your sorrows, you don't get a result of succeeding. That action leads to a hangover, or more sadness, or isolating yourself.

In order to have a different result (like cool opportunities pouring in), you have to change your frequency. You have to jump up to different thoughts and feelings. Like this: Instead of feeling sad and rejected, you feel hopeful. Whatever made you feel sad and rejected, doesn't take away from how awesome you are. You focus on that, and feel hopeful for the future. This leads to an action: "I think I'll shoot an email to that person I met a few months ago. Maybe that could lead to something." You send the email and that leads to a result: you book a meeting with this new connection.

When you access your Star Power and become the person who believes you're going to succeed, it leads to the most effective actions and the best results. You don't wait for the results to take the actions. So how do you do this? How do you become that person? How do you access your Star Power? At the very foundation, you need to think like a successful person. This might sound like faking it until you make it. But here's why it's not: you're not pretending to be successful. You're accessing greatness that is always innately inside you. You don't have to fake anything. All you need to do is connect to your inner being that knows you are incredible and worthy, even before you do anything. It's a feeling that you don't think you'll have until after you succeed. But that's just not true. You can feel those things right now.

Many people have this idea that Hollywood is like an exclusive club— one of those VIP-only clubs, of which you'll always be on the outside. One morning as I drove to work, I listened to Shonda Rhimes narrate her book, *The Year of Yes* (Shonda Rhimes has become one of the biggest creators in television, responsible for shows like *Grey's Anatomy* and *How To Get Away With Murder*). Deep into the third chapter, I had a thought: I feel far away from Shonda and her world. Listening to her read, it felt like I was on the outside of the Hollywood Club, and Shonda was on the inside. I think many people share this story—that their dreams are a club that's hard to get into and we spend most of our time with our faces glued to the windows, watching the glamor and wondering if we'll ever get to be a part of it. *Cue the "best friend" energy*

Feeling far away from it all, the Universe suddenly smacked me on the head and said, "Girl, you're crazy! Look around!" I couldn't help but laugh at the irony: That week I was working on the TV show *SMILF*, which filmed at Sunset Gower Studios, the actual headquarters of

Shondaland. As I drove onto the lot, *Scandal* was filming on the stages in front of me. Shonda's office (and parking spot) were to my left. Could I BE inside this club any more? (Said in my best Chandler voice.)

The whole being-on-the-outside concept is just a belief. Your dreams are not a club only open to the popular kids, or the VIP kids. There is room for you. When we buy into the belief that we're on the outside, that's where we'll stay. But that wall is an illusion. Successful people don't buy into that separation. They believe there is no obstacle they can't get through, and deep in their heart, they feel worthy of the success they want. This doesn't mean they don't have fears or doubts that creep in regularly. It simply means, they live their life from possibility, instead of *im*possibility. Your Star Power is your proverbial VIP badge and you don't need to wait for someone to give it to you. It's already yours, so come on in!

But most of us don't start there. Most of us grow up with messaging that insists our dreams are impossible. Maybe we believe others can succeed, but *we* can't. Maybe we're told we're not good enough. Maybe we don't feel worthy. By the time we're in our 20s, we have a plethora of experiences that have impacted our belief system. Some of us have had life-changing traumas, and most of us have experienced some kind of words or incidents that traumatically tore down our worth and weakened our self-esteem (my personal list is as long as a CVS receipt). Regardless of the cause, as we grow up, we have many beliefs that stop us from going after our dreams, or that get in the way of the success we desire. Those beliefs stop us from accessing our Star Power.

Therapy is an excellent avenue to work through these things. While therapy is often focused on the past and uncovering things we didn't realize were there, coaching is often focused on the future, giving action steps to move forward. That's what this next exercise is for. When you're ready to move forward, here's the exercise my clients go through (and I still use for myself):

## FROM FEAR TO DESIRE

Grab your list from Chapter 1. Now that you know everything you want to achieve in your life, it's time to face the fears that come with that list. Transforming those fears into positive affirmations is the most effective next step you can take to shift into your Star energy.

Get a piece of paper and draw a line down the middle to split the page in half. On the left hand side, I want you to write "Doubts and Fears". Leave the right side blank for now.

As you look at your list of dreams from Chapter 1, what comes up for you? On this left hand side, I want you to make a list of every fear or doubt that comes up when you think about your dreams. We want to let it all out, so don't hold back. It's also important that you go deep here. I know it may not be fun, but it's a necessary key to getting everything you want. Remember, there is no judgement here. It's okay to have these fears. It makes you human. There is nothing wrong with you, so let it all out!

Here are some common fears that have come up for my clients:
1. Fear of not being good enough
2. Fear it will never happen
3. Fear it won't last
4. Fear if they do succeed, it will interfere with other areas of their life (like relationships)
5. Fear of never having access to resources or connections

It's really common to have fears tied to worthiness and deservedness. Those are the two most common themes I see when my clients go through this process. You have to be really honest with yourself and self-aware to recognize that's what is underneath it all. So take your time with this. And please know that writing these down doesn't make them come true. All we're doing is digging beyond the surface to see what beliefs are floating around in your subconscious that could potentially sabotage your efforts with your dreams.

After you've finished this list, move on to the right side of the paper. At the top, write "Affirmations." This is where you're going to turn your fears into affirmations by flipping them to their opposite, so we can change the belief from sabotaging to supportive.

For an example, I'll go through the common list above. Beginning with the first fear: fear of not being good enough. If you believe you're not good enough, *what do you wish you believed?* We want to turn this into a positive affirmation that essentially states the opposite of the fear. So if I believed I wasn't good enough, I wish I believed that I *was* good enough. Now let's turn that into an affirmation. I might say, "I am good enough." That would state the opposite of the fear. Or, if I wanted this to be really powerful, I wouldn't use the word "enough" because it implies lack. So I might change this to, "I am worthy of my dreams *now!*" Or, "I have a gift that I'm meant to share with the world." Play around with it until you find what resonates with you.

Here are example affirmations for the rest of the common fears:
1. I am worthy of my dreams.
2. My success is inevitable. (This is my personal mantra.)
3. I create my own success. I can create it over and over again. I create my own reality. (And I would go on to say that success isn't some-

thing you find and can lose, it's something you create.)

4. My success will amplify all other areas of my life. As I feel more joy and achieve more goals, I'll strengthen my relationships and inspire those around me.

5. I'm always guided to the resources and connections I need. I am incredibly resourceful.

Once you have your two lists, I want you to look at them side-by-side. Imagine that these lists are two different people. The "Fears" list on the left is Person A. The "Affirmations" list on the right is Person B. What kind of outcome do you think Person A will have? If that list is their belief system, what kind of actions would they take? What kind of results would they get?

On the other side, what about Person B? If that list is their belief system, what kind of outcome will Person B have? What kind of actions will they take? What kind of results would they get?

It should be obvious at this point that Person A is likely going to struggle and Person B is likely to succeed. Our beliefs shape our outcomes, that's why we start here. Even though each of these people will have drastically different outcomes, the point of this exercise isn't to make you feel bad about having those fears. The truth is, you are Person A *and* Person B. It's totally okay that you have these fears, as I mentioned, it's what makes you human. You're not a robot, congratulations! It's not necessarily about getting rid of the fears. **It's really about making the affirmations louder.** We want that second list to be dominant. We want you to send your fears to the back seat of the car and let the affirmations be in the driver's seat. As Tony Robbins says, we learn to dance with the fears. Over time, the affirmations will become our beliefs. For now, as we move forward, we want to repeat these affirmations over and over to ourselves every day. We want to remind ourselves that we are worthy and we can do this.

After we do this, **it's all about our feelings.** You might be like, "Erica, I say 'I'm worthy of my dreams' but I don't actually believe it." I know. That's how this process works. The words aren't magical and don't necessarily make you believe them or feel them. But the feeling is what makes all the difference. Feelings create the vibrational energy we send out into the Universe. Words alone are not enough to change that vibration. This is where the real work begins. You have to say the affirmations until you feel them. I want you to feel worthy, even if it starts for only a moment. There are many ways to do this, and you should experiment to find what works for you. Here are ways that I do this:

1. **Visualization:** Try closing your eyes for a moment. Imagine you feel worthy. Picture yourself in a situation where you feel worthy. To go further, imagine you're living out your dream. Involve all of your senses (see, touch, smell, taste, hear). Be in the moment of your dream as clearly as you can, even if it's only for 5 minutes.

2. **Access the general feeling:** If you can't feel the feeling for this specific affirmation, recall a time in your life when you felt that feeling, even if it has nothing to do with your dreams. For example, maybe you felt confident the last time you did well on an exam. Try to remember that moment and access that feeling of confidence. Or do a task that usually makes you feel confident; when I first started coaching and my confidence wavered, I would work on a Graphic Design project because I felt super confident there. It's how I accessed the feeling, even if it pertained to a different topic.

3. **Change your physical state:** This is something Tony Robbins

often teaches, to change your body's position. If you're feeling unworthy, you may be sitting hunched over, making yourself small. If you felt worthy, you would be sitting tall or standing. Change your physical body positioning to match the feeling you want to feel. Your brain will connect to this. Smiling is also a great one that works, try to smile and not feel happy. I dare you.

4.   **Repeat the affirmations with intentional feeling:** Even if all you can muster is one minute of worthiness, over time that one minute will grow, and you'll soon believe that you can have this dream.

This is how you become the person you want to be, this is how you access your Star Power. In order to achieve your dreams, you're going to have to take risks—scary risks that are way outside of your comfort zone. The only way you'll do that is if you believe in yourself and you believe your dreams are possible. Stop playing the best friend. Stop waiting for a resume to prove your greatness. You are the leading person in your own life. You are the Star, now.

# Three

# THE 10 PILLARS OF A HIGH ACHIEVER

The third TV show I worked on was one of the most influential in my career because it's the show on which I got into the union (the Art Director's Guild). Ironically, it's also one of the worst experiences I've ever had in Hollywood. I hesitate to make that statement because I'm forever a glass-half-full person, and I have lots of fond memories from that show. It wasn't all horrible. I made some great friends and met some really cool people. But I also spent the last day crying in my car and feeling the most alone I had felt in a long time.

It was a new show on TBS, and I landed the job of Art Department PA (Production Assistant). It's the lowest on the totem pole, and everyone's starting point. As an Art PA, my job was to run errands and do other assistant-like tasks to help the Art Department run as smoothly as possible. For me, it was a placeholder until I could be what I really wanted: a Graphic Designer.

The show was about a fraternity at a college, so we actually filmed on a real college campus. The campus wasn't operating anymore, but our offices were in an old building that doubled as the fraternity. The Art Department was upstairs on the second floor, and the set was on the first floor, so every time they filmed a scene in the frat, we had to whisper and hold all the calls when the phone rang. As someone who was still relatively new to Hollywood, I freaking loved it. The only thing that would make me happier would be working as a Graphic Designer and not an assistant.

My boss on this show was also designing a second show, so he split his time between the two. This meant he wasn't in our office very often, but when he was, he was always supportive and kind. To this day, he is one of the best bosses I've ever worked for. Since he wasn't around much, the Art Director, his second-in-command was in charge. And for some reason this Art Director did not like me.

As per the last chapter, I was always BEing who I wanted to be. My dream was to be a Graphic Designer, and I told anyone who would listen. This was actually part of my strategy and led to a lot of people helping me along the way. I was clear on what I wanted, and I constantly asked people how to get there. This show was no exception. And because of this, the Set Designer decided to help me figure out how to get in the union.

This felt like a miracle, because when I asked people how to get into the union in the past, I would often get this answer: "Don't let the union know you want to get in. They protect their members and if it looks like you're going to take the job of one of their members, they won't have it. So whatever you do, don't call the union." This seemed so harsh, but I followed what they said. I didn't want to do anything "wrong" in Hollywood. Until one day on this show, the Set Designer said, "That's silly. I'm in the union, I'll call them and ask how a Graphic Designer gets in."

I don't know if my commitment to my dream threatened the Art Director somehow, or he felt I was going to take his job from him, but it was clear that he wasn't my biggest fan. Whenever I had to interact with him, he would speak condescendingly to me. I was always afraid to approach him, unless it was absolutely necessary.

That necessary moment came when I learned how to get into the union. The Set Designer who generously called the union on my behalf, was told that I only needed one day on the books as a Graphic Designer on a TV show, and then I could get in. If you work in Hollywood, then you know that is absolutely absurd, as most people need at least 30 days, and some positions require years. It's a long story why this was the case, but regardless, it was true at that time. I only needed one day of work on the payroll, and this was fantastic news because it's a relatively easy ask.

When my boss was in the office the next day, I told him this news and asked if there was a way that I could work one day as a Graphic Designer, and then continue my time as a PA. He graciously offered to ask the Producers and said it seemed like no big deal. I was ecstatic! All I wanted was to be in the union so I could officially work as a Graphic Designer and no longer need to be an assistant. The Producers agreed, and all my dreams were coming true! I was so excited and it felt so great to have such a supportive boss in this process. When the day arrived, I felt so cool. I was literally living my dream as a Graphic Designer for television, even if it was only for one day. At the end of that week, it was time to hand in our time cards. This was my ticket into the union. Once I had a pay stub that said "Graphic Designer" I was in! I took so much joy in filling out that time card. Little did I know, I was a few moments away from that joy being robbed.

Our boss wasn't there that day, so our time cards had to be signed by the second-in-command, the Art Director. My heart sank when I realized this. All I needed was that signature, and then I could officially apply to the union. Slowly, I walked to the Art Director's office. I handed him my time card, just like any other day, and it was added to the pile. Then, he said he wouldn't sign it. He refused.

I didn't understand. This was already approved by the producers (who are above the Art Director in the hierarchy of TV shows), and it was also approved by my boss, who was also his boss. His refusal was clearly personal. For some reason, he didn't want to help me get into the union. I had to wait for our boss to come back in order to get it signed. As a young person, new to Hollywood, I felt crushed. I had no idea why this person was blocking me from my dreams.

My sadness subsided when I finally got the paycheck. That one day of pay as a Graphic Designer was equivalent to what I made in an entire week as an assistant! I felt rich! And holy crap, this is what I will be making when I get into the union! Everything calmed down, until the last day.

As we were wrapping the show on the very last day, the Art Director decided to take the entire Art Department out to lunch to celebrate... everyone except me. He told me to pack up and go home early. The rest of the department were all great people, with whom I had grown close.

They were my friends...or at least "work friends." We spent countless hours together every day. And now, they were celebrating without me. I packed up my things and headed to my car. I'll never forget that final moment: Before driving away, I sat there, looking out my window, as I watched them walk across the street to the restaurants. A lump in my throat began to form, and before I knew it, I was sobbing. Full on ugly cry. I had no idea what I did to create this, and I felt so alone.

Now, ten years later, I know that hurt people hurt people. I didn't do anything wrong. In fact, when my boss found out all of this had happened, he apologized to me. He has also hired me as a Graphic Designer many times after that show, once I was in the union. What I've learned is that there will be many ups and downs in a dream pursuit. There will be obstacles, and good days, and opportunities, and rejections. The High Achiever (a.k.a. you!), needs a game plan through it all. The High Achiever needs to handle all of these moments intentionally and carefully, in a way that effectively keeps them on the path to success. That's why I developed the Ten Pillars of the High Achiever. Being successful doesn't mean that obstacles never arise. But the successful person approaches them in a very specific way. It's Star Power through and through.

And since we're focused on BEing the successful person now, I want these pillars to be your armor. These pillars represent the mindset of a successful person. They show you the most effective thinking for a dream pursuit. Successful people think differently. They make decisions differently. These ten pillars are everything.

Whenever I share these pillars with my clients, they always say, "Oh, yes! This makes perfect sense! I love this!" Then the journey happens and the pillars go out the window. I know these ten pillars sound nice, in theory. But these pillars are not meant for theory. They're meant for real life. Every time real life happens, I remind my clients to go back to the pillars.

So here's what I suggest: go through these ten pillars, and **memorize them**. Reread them again and again. Whenever obstacles pop up in your pursuit, go back to the pillars. They are the guiding light that will bring you back to your Star Power. If you take anything away from this book, take these pillars. Use them, not just for your career, but for any dream you have. You can think like a successful person anytime you want. You have it at your fingertips.

## THE 10 PILLARS
## PILLAR 1: ABUNDANCE ALWAYS

Many dream pursuits preach scarcity. People love spreading the message that there are not enough opportunities, and the chance that you may succeed is incredibly rare. That's a cute story, but I'm not here for it. Successful people don't believe in scarcity, they believe in abundance. The truth is, there are an abundance of opportunities available to you at any given time.

My absolute favorite Abraham Hicks quote says, "People get to the dock and think they missed their boat. But there is always another one coming." When you focus on a shortage of opportunities, you put a lot of pressure on anything that comes your way. That pressure creates anxiety and affects your performance. It creates an energy of desperation like, "Wow! I got an opportunity! I better not blow this because this may be the only shot I get." Ick.

When you believe in abundance, it takes the pressure off of any single opportunity. It also leads to consistent strategic moves—moves that you wouldn't take after a rejection if you believed another opportunity was never going to come. If you lost an opportunity and were completely crushed, you may never get back up. But there is always another opportunity available. Abundance creates motivation to keep going and keep trying.

This is also important when it comes to competition. Abundance says there is room for all of us. We all have our own unique gifts to share with the world that no one can replicate. Opportunities, resources, support, is all abundantly here for us. Believe in it, and you'll see it. There is no limit on what you can create for yourself. You can have it all, as it's all always available.

## PILLAR 2: DECISIONS COME FROM DESIRE, NOT FEAR

Most people make fear-based decisions. But you're not most people! Successful people make decisions that support their dreams, even if it feels scary. For example, let's say you have contact information for a person who could potentially help you with your dream. But you're scared to contact them. You don't want to bother them and you're scared they won't want to help. So you decide not to contact them. That is a decision made from fear. The successful person may still have those fears, but they contact the person anyway because it could help their dream. This also happens on a grander scale, when it comes to taking a big leap, investing in yourself, or taking any kind of risk. We'll continue to talk about risk throughout this book, but I can not stress enough how crucial it is. If you're consistently making decisions out of fear, that means you're not taking any risks. And when you're not taking any risks, you're not reaping any rewards.

Whenever you make a decision, pause, and ask yourself: Am I making this decision out of fear? Or does this decision help me move forward?

## PILLAR 3: OBSTACLES ARE OPPORTUNITIES TO PIVOT

I can't even say that P word without immediately picturing Ross Geller and that couch. When you hit an obstacle, be like Ross Geller and yell PIVOT!

Seriously. Obstacles usually feel awful in the moment, but I promise you, they are opportunities in disguise. Even the most successful people have had many challenges along their paths. My cousin was in a car accident years ago, hit by a drunk driver. He survived, but his recovery took eight months, and during that time he decided to write his first full-length feature, which went on to be nominated for four Oscars. A damaging car accident is a pretty big obstacle, but my cousin used it as an opportunity to create something amazing. Obstacles are part of the journey and there is nothing you can do to avoid them (except choose not to pursue your dream). It's not about avoiding obstacles, it's about what you do with them.

Remember that ABC Family show I mentioned? The one that was my best experience ever? Well, before that, I was on a TV show that didn't go so well. I finished out the season, but I wasn't asked back when they returned for the next season. I knew I wasn't going to be asked back. My ego was crushed. It was a show that went on for a long time, so if I was asked back, I could have had job stability for many years. It was a pretty big obstacle. But because that door closed, another one opened on that ABC Family show. I believed in abundance, and knew there had to be another job out there for me. I pivoted. And I landed on Chasing Life. If that obstacle never happened, I never would have had that great experience and created friendships that have become like family.

Successful people are solution-oriented rather than problem-oriented.

Most people, when faced with an obstacle, focus on the problem. They focus on it so much, they can't even see a solution. All they see is a dead end. The High Achiever believes in solutions. When they hit an obstacle, they shift into the energy of the solution. They don't see a dead end, they see an opportunity to pivot. Do you know about the hidden arrow in the FedEx logo? In the white space between the E and the x, is the shape of an arrow. There is also a baking spoon in the lowercase e in Fed. I knew about the arrow, but when I heard about the spoon, my mind was blown. "Omg! It was there the whole time and I never noticed!" See where I'm going here? Solutions, or opportunities to pivot, are always there when you know to look for them. People who are problem-oriented never see those solutions, even if they are right there in front of them just like the arrow and the spoon.

Obstacles are inevitable. But so is your success (spoiler alert from Pillar #7!). Believe in ways to pivot, and you'll see ways to pivot. See them as scavenger hunt clues. When one pops up, it's going to lead you to your next clue. In my experience, the obstacles have always led to something so much better.

## PILLAR 4: EVENTS ARE NEUTRAL, WE DECIDE WHAT THEY MEAN

The stories we tell ourselves dictate everything: how we feel, what actions we take, and the results we get. We're really good at creating stories when something goes wrong (or when we're rejected). The moment we are faced with a rejection, the conversation in our mind begins, "I'm not good enough. They didn't like me. I'm not likable. I'm not talented. This is never going to happen. This won't work. I guess I'm not meant for this." Sound familiar?

I can tell you this for sure, we are all really freaking talented at bullshit.

Am I right?! Those stories we tell ourselves are not the truth. They are 100% bullshit. Fake news. Fiction. But we are pretty convincing, so we believe them with all our heart. The real truth is this: anything that goes "wrong" on your journey, or any time you're rejected...those events are neutral. They are not good, they are not bad. We assign a meaning to them. We decide if it's good or bad. We fill in the blanks with why we think it happened. And those stories cause us to spiral. That spiral can send us into depression and sadness, and sometimes last for years. It becomes a reason to stop trying. The first show that I worked on got canceled after the first season, and suddenly I was out of work and back to the drawing board. With almost no connections, I had a really hard time finding work again. I went through 9 months of depression, telling myself that the Universe was punishing me. I used to cry in my room and wonder why I didn't deserve success. It was the negative meaning I attached to struggling to find work. When in reality, from an objective perspective, I simply didn't know enough people in the industry yet to book work right away.

The High Achiever stops engaging in the fictional storytelling. They don't attach a negative meaning to a neutral event without facts and data to back it up. Events are neutral. You are the only one who gets to decide if you're meant for this. It's not up to fate, it's a decision.

## PILLAR 5: HOW YOU VIEW YOUR PAST

If you've made it this far in the book, you know that I've had some bad experiences on my journey. You've probably had some, too. Whether it's someone mistreating you, an opportunity not working out, or just a bunch of struggle, we've all had moments that make us pause before trying again. When I was younger, I dated a handful of guys who treated me poorly. (It was mostly my fault, as I just didn't love myself enough to ask for what I truly wanted.) Since then, I've definitely had the fear that when I date again, I'll have the same experience. Even though I've done the work with a therapist and a life coach, and I've never been happier by myself before, there is still that thought that my future will look exactly the same as my past. But that's just not true. As long as my energy is different, I'm not going to recreate the same bad experiences. My past will not dictate my future potential.

I know it's common to have this fear—that whatever bad experiences you've had, you're sure they're going to repeat. You're so sure that you stop yourself from pursuing it again, out of self protection. Maybe the last time you put yourself out there, you were rejected. Or maybe you lost a job. Or maybe you sent a resume and it wasn't even considered. And now, you're afraid to try again. I want you to know that your past absolutely does not define your future. It does not dictate what will happen. Your potential is infinite, regardless of what has happened. And remember, you create your own reality. So you get to choose how your future will look.

## PILLAR 6: HOW YOU VIEW YOUR PRESENT

This is one of the more challenging Pillars, so get ready! How You View Your Present is all about focusing on the process, not the result.

When we plant a seed, it's really hard to be patient and wait for the flower to appear. I mean, at least for me. When I want something, I pull a Veruca Salt and want it NOW! But we know that a seed doesn't become a flower right away. It needs water, sunlight, and soil. If you get really good at watering that seed and taking care of it, it's going to blossom eventually. You need to focus on the process and get really good at it, trusting that the result will inevitably come.

What happens if you sit next to the seed and stare at it and yell,

"FLOWER, WHERE THE F*#K ARE YOU??!" That somehow prolongs the flower. Because now you're angry and annoyed and disappointed, so you skip a day or two with watering and suddenly you're not so good at the process anymore. When you focus on lack, you get more lack. When you worry about the result and spend time complaining that it's not here yet, it affects your process (or your actions). You're not as good at watering your dreams.

Focus on getting really damn good at your process. So whether that's connecting with people, making an ask, refining your interview skills, or brushing up on your marketing, get really good at it. When you're really good at those things, it's inevitable that your result will come. Be in the present moment, follow the steps, and arm yourself with your Star Power. You've got this!

## PILLAR 7: HOW YOU VIEW YOUR FUTURE

Your success is inevitable. Period. That's what you need to believe. Whenever I pursue a dream, like trying to get a book deal for this book, I don't have time to waste even considering that it won't happen. I only have time to believe it's going to happen. Anything less will delay my success.

When you believe your success is inevitable, you take the risks. You make the ask. You keep going in the face of rejection. Because you know. You know it's going to happen, so you always move forward. This belief completely changes the game. Imagine if you were shaky on this. Imagine if you thought, "I mean, I hope it happens. But I don't really know if it will." What actions would you take from that place? What would you feel inspired to do? It's a half-assed process.

Say it with me, "My success is inevitable." Add this to your Affirmation list if it's not on there already. This is where faith comes in. You have to believe in something before you have any proof. You have to believe in your dream like Santa Clause, knowing in your heart that it's coming, even though you haven't seen it. Success is a decision. It's not up to fate, it's up to you. If you believed **for certain** that your dream was going to happen, what would you do?

"Those who are certain of the outcome can afford to wait, and wait without anxiety." - *A Course In Miracles*

## PILLAR 8: RESPOND INSTEAD OF REACT

Just like Pillar #2 tells you not to make decisions based in fear, Pillar 8 doesn't want you to make decisions from an emotional state.

When a rejection or obstacle happens, it's important that you allow yourself to feel the feelings that come up. Let yourself cry. As we already established, you're not a robot. So it's OK to be human and feel the emotions that come along with a situation. In fact, it's healthy to let them out. I'm totally a crier. I cry all the time. I fully practice Pillar #4, and I don't let myself stay there, in those negative stories. But I do let myself release it. What I don't do, though, is make decisions from that state.

It's easy to want to make rash decisions about your next steps when you're feeling emotional. But that often leads to making decisions from fear. You can have your reaction. But don't respond until you've calmed down and can make decisions that support your dream (i.e. don't decide to give up on your dreams when you're midway through a pint of Ben and Jerry's, sniffling through tears).

P.S. The more you do this work, the shorter the time it will take to feel inspired again. Instead of feeling sad for a month, you'll feel sad for a day. Growth has its benefits!

## PILLAR 9: YOU ARE CEO, THIS IS YOUR BUSINESS

This one might sound a little weird, but hear me out. Think about your dream right now. What is it? There is a good chance that right now it only exists as a hobby, not a tangible dream. But I want it to be tangible for you. I want you to have it and live it out. For that to happen, you have to start thinking about it as something tangible, and not a fluffy concept. When you think about your dream as a business, as something more serious in terms of tangibility, it's going to manifest that way.

Think of the different aspects a business has: marketing, accounting, sales, creation. While not everyone of those will apply to every dream, they are still concepts that can help you move out of hobby mode and into reality mode. Chapter 13 will dive into marketing and how to sell yourself, but as far as this Pillar is concerned, there is one area that every dream can benefit from learning: investing.

Every business has 3 types of costs:
1. Startup
2. Maintenance
3. Uplevel

Startup costs cover any investments required to get your dream off the ground. This might include equipment, training, or even moving to a specific city. A photographer may need to invest in a camera, a doctor needs to invest in education, and a director might move to Los Angeles to get connected with a community. Maintenance costs cover maintaining your dream. For example, a realtor may have to renew their license every 4 years. Or an actor may have to get their hair colored every few months. Uplevel costs cover investments that help you move up to a new level. Like a teacher getting their Masters to qualify for a higher level position, or an entrepreneur hiring a publicist to help them reach a larger audience.

I know money can be a scary thing (that's why I've got you covered with an entire chapter on it, so stay tuned!), but it's also an important part of taking your dream into reality. Thinking of your dream as a business is going to make all the difference. You are the CEO of your dream so it's time you took charge of it and steered it into the direction of fully realized.

## PILLAR 10: THE RUTHLESS BOUNCER

These Pillars will put you on the path to success. Like I mentioned earlier, they sound great in theory, but what about when real life happens?

The hardest part is not letting other people's words break this wall down. Because the Negative Nancys are out there and they will voice their doubts in very convincing ways. That's why you need to be ruthless about what you allow into your mind and energy. These Pillars set you up for success and the moment you slip back into Nancy's limiting beliefs, your success is delayed.

Here's how your subconscious mind works: whatever is stored in there, your mind thinks is the absolute truth (kinda like those people who argue on the internet and aren't capable of seeing any other side...they insist their opinion is right and everyone else is wrong). Let's go back to the FedEx example. If your subconscious mind only sees the orange and purple letters, it believes that is the truth and nothing else exists. It doesn't matter that the arrow and spoon do exist in the white space—if your mind only believes in the letters, it will only see the letters (until you show it proof). So the information stored in your subconscious will always be reflected back to you in your physical world. You'll see whatever is stored in there.

You will always find what you're looking for because your mind is wired to find proof that matches the "truth" inside it. Just like the FedEx logo, if you've stored "I'm not good enough" in your subconscious, it will be reflected back to you in your life. You'll constantly have experiences that prove this to be true, that you're not good enough. And it won't just be random experiences that fall in your lap and confirm you're not good enough. Your mind will actually lead you to create those moments.

The good news is that it works this way no matter what is in there. So if you believe that you are good enough, you'll seek out experiences that prove that true. Can you see the importance of what is stored in your subconscious mind? It plays a significant role in your actions and the results you see. That's why you need to be ruthless about what you allow in there.

Picture this: your subconscious mind is a club—an exclusive club with a bouncer at the door. There is music pumping and people (a.k.a. your thoughts) dancing, having a grand old time. It's no wonder that everyone wants to get in there! But, alas, there is that huge bouncer standing outside the club, deciding who gets in. Guess who that bouncer is? It's your conscious mind! (When I put that exclamation mark, I suddenly felt like this was an episode of Sesame Street and I was really excited to explain this to you. I'm cool, I swear!)

How does your conscious mind decide who gets into the hopping Subconscious Club? It's all based on truth. Let's play this out: Let's say

44

you're hanging out with Nancy and Nancy says to you, "That dream you're trying to go after is really hard. It probably won't happen." Oh Nancy, always with the encouraging words, right?! Well, in that moment, you have a choice. You can choose to believe what Nancy said, or you can choose to reject it as truth. That's your Conscious Bouncer dude, deciding if this statement gets to come into the party. If you decide what Nancy said is true, then it's in! Past the ropes, no cover needed, in it goes! If you decide it's not true, then it's not getting in the club and you just won this round of Your Dream vs. Disbelievers. Wooooooo!

Let's say, just for example's sake, because I know, of course, that you would never do this...but let's just say that you believe Nancy. You're like, "Yup. That's True!" Your Conscious Bouncer dude let's that statement into the club, and then what? What did we say about how the subconscious works? That's right. We said whatever is stored in there will be reflected back to you. So now, welcome to the fun game of struggle and defeat! (I wish you could hear my Announcer voice. I swear it makes this scientific learning way more hip.)

Now, every time you put yourself out there, you'll be met with struggle. Because you've accepted the truth that "this probably won't happen." And if I'm being super honest, you'll most likely take less risks, and you'll end up with actions that will definitely prove Nancy's theory—because, remember, your mind will actually lead you to create circumstances that support this "truth." One example of this I see in Hollywood, is when actors take day jobs that are during the day (like a 9-5 job). Auditions happen during the day, so if you have a 9-5 job you can't audition. You're essentially setting yourself up for failure. But if you believe that acting is hard and it probably won't happen, you take actions that prove this to be true. And our mind creates lots of creative excuses of why this action is a good idea: "Well, this 9-5 job is in a production company, so maybe they will hire me as an actor on one of their productions!" They are often far-fetched ideas, but we are really good at convincing ourselves of our excuses. Because we have to prove the Subconscious stuff true.

Another way this commonly plays out is if you're focused on getting a promotion at your day job. If your dream requires a day job of some sort, for example, if you want to be an entrepreneur but have to stay in your 9-5 until you can afford to leave, when you believe in your success, you see the day job as a means to an end. You know it's just there to support you while you work on your dream. But if you believe Nancy, then you do things like try to get a promotion at your day job, where you're putting more energy into succeeding at the day job instead of succeeding at your dream.

Sometimes Nancy's words are more nuanced and less obvious. So how do you figure out if it's something your bouncer should accept? An easy way to evaluate is by asking this question: Does this limit me in any way? Or, does it stop me from taking an action? Does it stop me from moving forward? Does it feel discouraging? Ask yourself these questions before letting the bouncer make its decision.

As you can see, your mindset is everything. Your beliefs are everything. Now that you have these 10 pillars, it's imperative that you become ruthless about what else you allow in. You can do this. You are amazing. Your success is inevitable. Anything less is not comin' in da club.

*Four*

# THE LUCKY BREAK
# FORMULA

I was listening to one of my favorite podcasts as I drove from Malibu back to the eastside (I know, could I be any more LA?), when I heard a line that is way too common, in my opinion. Two Hollywood stars were chatting about their success and one of them said, "So much of it is luck." The other chimed in with agreement. I almost slammed on my breaks in disagreement as my intuition screamed, "NO!"

I mean, who am I to disagree with two wildly successful Hollywood stars, especially on their perspectives of their own journey? But for me, it's exactly that—a *perspective*. In my own decade of working in Hollywood and an additional five years coaching Hollywood creatives, I've learned that "luck" is a perspective, not a fact. Together, myself and my clients have booked over 60 television shows and films, and not an ounce of luck when into it, at least that's our *perspective*.

Luck is an illusion. It's a word people use when they can't explain the role they've played. I never use this word to describe my own success because I know that I created it. While I can't control who will say "Yes" or when it will be said, I *can* control everything else—what I do, the risks I take, the perseverance I live through, and the drive I have. A door will eventually open because I've decided it will. That belief drives everything I do.

When I broke into Hollywood, a guy named Henry helped me. I didn't know him before. I cold messaged him on Facebook (he was one of about 150 people I cold contacted). Henry was the one who got me that first interview with Tim and Jim. Whenever I share this, people always respond with, "Wow, you got so lucky! You're so lucky you found Henry!" But it wasn't luck at all. It was persistence and numbers. And, honestly, it's a little insulting to think it was due to luck and not the work I did. If Henry didn't help me, I would have cold contacted 150 more people until someone else did. I believed in my success and I wouldn't have stopped until I found my way in.

When we look up to mentors who say they were successful because of luck, it leaves no roadmap for us. It also leads us down a path of questioning our self-worth: *Am I worthy of luck? They must have been special, and I'm not.* Luck puts us in a passive position, it leaves us waiting. But here's the thing—as I've said, we create our own reality. And doors opening is something that can absolutely be reverse engineered. Luck is one perspective, but it's one I choose not to buy into because I live in a reality where my success is inevitable. I choose a perspective that says I am capable, worthy, and have the power to receive opportunities. I'm not wishing, hoping, praying that one day I'll get my lucky break. I'm creating. I'm acting. I'm doing.

I hope you start to see that this book is here to give you your power back. I want to show you that we can control a lot, and those things we can control have a massive impact on the results we get. I know how disheartening it is to hear people attribute their success to luck because then it feels like no matter what you do, it doesn't matter...there is some greater force out there that determines our fate and has little to do with our actions. I do believe in a greater force, but I believe it works with us, rather than solo. And I believe it wants us to win. But the only way it can help us win is if we do our part, too.

Luck is a door opening, that's all! So how can we create that for ourselves? As Jack Canfield says, "Success leaves clues." So all we have to do is follow the clues. All we have to do is reverse engineer how doors have opened for other people. When we break it down, there are four clear elements that lead to "luck": 1) Energy; 2) Strategy; 3) Risk; 4) Opportunity. If luck is just a door opening, then we need to focus on finding the doors and doing everything we can to get one of them to open. The four elements do exactly that.

As you'll see in a moment, all four are imperative. If you get lazy on one of them, doors won't open. Consider these four like your combination code that unlocks a door. Your Energy, Strategy, and Risk, unlocks Opportunity.

Everyone thinks that strategy is the most important thing. Here's the truth: strategy is ONE OF the most important things. It's the "How." It's the tactics, it's the plan, it's *almost* everything. But it's only one of the numbers on that combination lock. It won't open the door all on its own.

Remember how a little boy might pull a little girl's ponytail if he liked her? Let's call that ponytail pulling, his *strategy*.

How did this strategy come about? It started with a thought: *I like Sally.* That thought turns into a belief: *I believe Sally can be my girlfriend.* That belief turns into a strategy: *I'll pull Sally's hair so she pays attention to me.*

Now, let's ignore the fact that this is a terrible strategy, for the moment. What would happen if we took that same scenario and changed the belief?

The thought: *I like Sally.*
The belief: *I'm not good enough to date Sally.*
The strategy: *No action is taken to connect with Sally.*

See where I'm going here?

Your strategy is born from your beliefs. While your strategy is incredibly important, it won't lead to "lucky breaks" if your energy isn't setting you up for success. The first element of this formula cannot be ignored. All of the strategic moves you make will be because of your energetic state. Period. You want doors to open? You want more opportunities? You want *better* opportunities? Start with the first element:

## ELEMENT #1: ENERGY
Your Energy is:
- Your belief system
- Your vibration
- Your feelings tied to your beliefs

It's the culmination of how you're feeling about your pursuit. In very basic terms, **you need to believe that what you're going after is possible, and you need to be excited about the possibilities.** When you believe this will happen, you'll create a powerful strategy. And when you *feel good* about it all, you'll receive the inspired ideas that make your strategy unstoppable.

Think about the last time you had a really great day. You know, that day where you felt so happy and inspired. What actions did you take? What risks did you feel inspired to take? Now think about the last time you had a pretty crummy day. What actions did you take then? Did you feel inspired to take any risks? Let's be honest: a shitty day where you're chained to your bed binging Netflix because you were just rejected is probably not the day you cold email 150 people. It's simple: **feeling good leads to good ideas.**

And there is science behind this, it's not just theory. You know that girl on Instagram who is always saying things like, "oh my goooooooddd, hashtag summer vibes!!" It's the "Rosé all day," girl with the perfectly curated (and heavily filtered) photo of a wine glass in a pool against a summer sky. That "Summer vibes" phrase paints a clear picture: it's the vibration of summer. Cause it's all about the *vibration*. Literally, energy vibrating. We all vibrate energy and that energy attracts other people with a similar vibration. Think about your "Friend vibe!" being totally different than that other dude's "Friend vibe." You know when you have that feeling that certain friend groups just wouldn't mesh well with other friend groups? That's because of mismatched vibrations.

So, back to you, and your vibes. What ARE your vibes? Are you like, total Boss Babe vibes? Or are you like, total Negative Nancy vibes? Whatever vibration you choose to put out is going to attract people (like connections!) and experiences that match that vibration. The energy that vibrates from you will connect to energy vibrating from others. So it's important to be intentional about that vibration. Because whatever energy you put out is going to impact the strategic ideas you pursue (and the people you then meet).

As you're probably beginning to see, these chapters are building upon each other. Chapters 1-3 have prepared you for this moment. They've helped you cultivate positive, sparkly energy about your big dream. You've got this first element down. *High five!* But as I've said before, how you implement this in the real world (outside of this book) is everything.

When we focus on all the bad stuff like:
- Why is it taking so long?
- Ugh, it's happening for my friends and not for me!
- Will this ever happen for me???

...All of that stuff expands. **Because what we focus on expands.** That's why we need our Energy to be positive and strong. We want that to expand. A note: we want our Energy to be legitimately positive, and not manufactured. The Universe knows when you're faking it.

## ELEMENT #2: STRATEGY

Luck doesn't happen when you're sitting on your couch doing nothing. You need to create a plan to achieve what you want. You need steps to take that will get you closer to your dream. That's your Strategy.

Your Energy will lead you to your Strategy. It will guide you to resources, tools, mentors, and actions. The plan you create (which I'll show you how to do in Chapter 7—what a cliffhanger, baby!) will be **intentional.** An intentional Strategy, one that purposefully leads you to the doors you want to knock on, is the second element in this formula.

## ELEMENT #3: RISK

And the most important thing about your Strategy is the third element: Risk.

Risk is the proverbial door you knock on. Your Strategy leads to the risks you choose to take. It seems like common sense, but most people aren't doing it. Taking risks is the only way you'll get any door open. If you're not putting yourself in a position to be rejected, you're not putting yourself in a position to get a "Yes." And that's all a risk is: putting yourself in a position to get a "Yes." It's putting yourself out there. It's 100% outside your comfort zone, which is why most people skip this part...and then complain when nothing happens.

People are scared of knocking. They're scared of failing, they're scared of being rejected. But not living your dream is so much scarier.

If you feel like you haven't had many opportunities lately, take a look at your risks. Have you taken any? When was the last time? When you take risks consistently, doors will open consistently. It's that simple.

## ELEMENT #4: OPPORTUNITY

I want you to think of Opportunity as something you create, not something you're waiting for. When you're living in a high vibrational energy and you strategically pursue what you want while taking risks and making the ask everyday, **opportunities** are guaranteed to be created.

It's like a recipe: mix your Energy base with a good helping of Strategy, and sprinkle in the strong taste of Risk, and you're bound to pull an Opportunity cake out of the oven. We don't always know how that opportunity will turn out, but now that you have the recipe, you can bake up as many as you need until one takes.

This is how luck is created. You shouldn't take a passive role in your career. You should be active because so much more is possible than you realize. So this is it. Your Energy leads to your Strategy, leads to the Risks you take, leads to Opportunities.

Can you see how you can create your own "luck"?

And maybe you're thinking, "But Erica, I can't control whether or not someone says 'Yes' to me. And that's where the luck really is." That's partly true. You can't control who says "Yes" to you, or when it happens. But you *can* control your Energy, Strategy, and Risk, which will inevitably lead to opportunities. The more you do this, the more opportunities you'll get. The more opportunities you get, the more chances you'll have that someone will say "Yes." It becomes a numbers game, and then it's just math! Your success is absolutely inevitable. A door will open. That "Yes" will come. Because, math.

# Five

# YOUR 5 BESTIES (AND WORSTIES)

O ne time, many years ago, I feel like I had an LA experience that confirms what outsiders think of this city. Which is kind of weird, because I haven't found many of the stereotypes to be true. I've met some really great, genuine people in LA. I've met people who support my dreams and actually want to help me. I'm constantly surrounded by people who are working incredibly hard for their dream (take that, East Coast!). But this time, I felt a little out of place.

My friend was invited to a launch party for a new jewelry line at her friend's store in Beverly Hills. I got to tag along and I was pretty excited to go. It was a small jewelry store, but there was a mini red carpet and flowing wine, and cameras flashing every few minutes. The glamour of a "launch party" has always been fun for me. I remember attending the premiere party for Glee when it first premiered and thought it was the coolest thing ever.

As the jewelry party got going and more people trickled in, I started to notice something...many of the women in attendance had similar faces. I know that sounds really weird, but that's the best way I can explain it! Even for someone who has lived in Los Angeles for over a decade, a city with the latest skincare offerings and aging solutions, I'm still pretty naive when it comes to Botox and plastic surgery. I guess you can take the girl out of Philly, but you can't take the Philly out of this girl.

Let me give this disclaimer: I don't judge anyone who chooses to get Botox or plastic surgery. I think people should do whatever makes them feel good, and that's a personal choice. More power to you, sister! Go for it! All I'm saying is that, as I looked around, I felt out of place. Nobody looked like me. Nobody had distinct facial features that seemed specific to them. Again, no shame. I just felt like I didn't belong.

Have you ever had a similar experience? Where you walk into a room and feel like you don't belong? I'm not talking about self-worth right now, I'm talking about entering a group of people and seeing that they all seem to fit together, but you're the square peg in the round hole. Like, if I walked into a group of super fit people I would immediately feel insecure, like I didn't belong. It's not that I'm horribly out of shape, but I'm not counting every macro and measuring my body fat every month.

Do you know why this happens? Why the fit people hang out with other fit people? Or the Botox people hang out with the Botox people? It's actually pretty simple: people connect with whom they have something in common. Makes sense, right?

Think about your closest friends circle. What do you have in common? Do you dress similarly? Do you have a common hobby or interest? Do you shop at similar places? Are you all Whole Food people or Costco people? Are you Target people or Chanel people? If you were to list everything you have in common with your closest friends, I bet you would find a huge list. I bet you eat similarly or have similar eating habits. I bet you have similar money spending habits. I bet you have similar weights. I bet you do similar activities on the weekends. I bet you watch similar shows. And I bet even your income is similar.

Jim Rohn says we are the average of the five people we spend the most time with. Literally, the average. So, for example, if you added up all of your incomes and divided it by 5 (to get the average) that would be the average income for the group. This makes sense if we think about what draws us together in the first place. It's not just things we have in common, but things we have in *comfortable*. (I was trying to be clever with that phrasing, just let me have it, OK?!)

Your comfort zone is the average of the five people you spend the most time with. Whatever you feel comfortable doing is probably similar to what your close friends feel comfortable doing. I want to tell you why this information could change your life: Think about this dream you want. The million dollars, the Oscar, the new business, the trip to the moon. Do any of your friends have it? Are they close? Since you are the average of the five people you spend the most time with, what is that average? Is it an average you're excited and happy about? Or an average that feels limiting?

In our tight friends circle, it's not just the *things* we have in common. It's also our thoughts. We think similarly to our friends circle. And those thoughts can either elevate us or keep us where we are. I have one group of friends where I'm let off the hook with my dreams and risks and thoughts. I can be my old self and I won't be judged because they have similar thoughts. I also have another group of friends where I can only be my best self. They don't tolerate limited thinking. It doesn't mean I have to be perfect all the time or can't mess up. It just means they elevate me. They also make more money than me and approach situations differently because they're a notch above the energy I've been living. Without the new group of friends, I might stay where I am. The old group of friends are my comfortable circle. So there, I stay comfortable.

If you want to be a millionaire, and your five closest friends average $50,000 a year, you're going to have to look outside your circle for advice. While there is absolutely nothing wrong with making $50k a year, someone at that income level won't know how to get $1 million dollars a year.

Who you surround yourself with is going to have a major impact on whether or not you achieve this dream. Think of all the work you've done so far with this book. Those 10 pillars you now embrace. The stronger belief in yourself and your dream. What will happen when you bring this conversation to your closest friends? Will they support it and want to know more? Or will they doubt it and bring you back to "reality?" (P.S. *Their* reality.)

Think of your dream like a newborn baby. You have to care for it and support it. You're not going to introduce it to a million people until it's older and stronger. Their immune system is still fragile, so you can't introduce anyone who's sick. This baby is precious and you need to protect it. You also need to seek out people (and books and advice) that can help you with it. People who have been through it and know how to take care of it and help it grow healthy. Get the picture?

The people around you will affect your dream and you have to decide who is best for it. This doesn't mean you have to go out and break up with all your friends. It just means that you want to be consciously aware of the conversations you have on a daily basis, and it's good to invite in people who can elevate you. Take inventory of your circle. Make note of the conversations or averages that may keep you where you are. Think about the energy you want to create for yourself. Embody that energy and see what friendships shift. Set the intention to elevate your average. As you begin to uplevel, whatever you used to tolerate will no longer be tolerable. Things that used to annoy you or felt a little irritating, will now become unbearable. That can be circumstances, a job, or even relationships. Take note of the friendships that become difficult to tolerate as you move through the internal work in this book.

## WHEN PEOPLE DON'T BELIEVE IN YOUR VISION

The thing with being a Visionary, and seeing something grand for your life, is that you're going to encounter people who just don't see it. As we've already established, this says nothing about you and your potential, and everything about the limiting beliefs those other people possess. But what do you do when it's your family? When it's your mom or dad or sibling? Especially for artists, it can be pretty common to have unsupportive parents. As Gary Vaynerchuk often explains, our parents come from a different generation where education and stable jobs were the coveted pedestal. Most of the time, our parents want us to succeed and be happy and they believe that can only happen one way. So if we stray from that path, they don't support it. They fear that we are hurting ourselves and sabotaging our potential for the life they want for us. It comes from a good place, but it can be soul-crushing, nevertheless.

When you feel like you're meant for something, like this dream is your purpose that you must fulfill, you have no choice but to pursue it. That necessity, pitted against the desire to make your parents proud, can feel like an impossible battle. We also tend to attach love to pride, so there's the fear that our parents won't love us unconditionally if we pursue a dream that goes against what they want. And since our deepest desires are to be seen and loved and heard, when it feels like that is threatened, we internally collapse. And, oh my gosh, while we're on the floor, wiping our tears feeling rejected by our own parents, we're supposed to be super strong and full of energy to put ourselves out there and risk everything? HEEEELLLLLPPPP!!!!!

I know. This is real. But let's talk about it because this dream of yours isn't going away. I want to pick you up off the floor, wipe your tears, give you a gigantic hug, and tell you, "You've got this." There are bound to be people who don't support your vision. That's a given. But what really matters is how we chose to react to that lack of support. It's easier when a stranger thinks your dream is crazy than when a family member does because we don't need love from the stranger. Sure, we may all want to be liked by strangers, but it's different than the deep love we expect from our family.

Any time we feel triggered or upset by something, it usually reflects our own insecurities about that topic. When we uncover why we feel triggered, it can help us move forward. An old coach of mine gave this great analogy—I call it the Green Hair Analogy. If someone in your family said to you, "Hey! Your hair is green!" when, in fact your hair is blonde or brown or red or gray or any color that isn't green, you probably wouldn't be upset. You might laugh at the absurdity. But it wouldn't upset you because **you know it's not true.**

When something does upset you, it's because part of you thinks it is true. If your family member said, "Your hair looks ugly," this might upset you if, deep down, you feared your hair was ugly. Make sense? So let's apply it to your dream. When your parents or family members don't support your dream, *why does it trigger you?* It could be, because, deep down, you doubt that you can do this. So when your family doubts you can do this, it triggers that insecurity. Your family is supposed to be the people who know you the best. And if the people who know you the best are saying that this isn't going to work for you and you should do something else for a living, then there must be truth to it.

That's where the pain comes from. If we dig beneath the surface of, "It's hard to do this without support," we find the real heart of the pain. Ideally, we want to get to a place where our family not supporting our dream is the equivalent of our family thinking we have green hair— something silly in which we find no truth. But, holy crap, how do we ever get to that point?

So much of what you've read so far is part of the key. Your freedom from this pain will come when you truly believe your success is inevitable and no one will shake you. It doesn't have to be that perfectly wrapped up in a pretty bow...it might be messier than that. But it is the goal, and the more you work on getting there, the easier it becomes.

There are two other pieces to this that are worth exploring: significance and identity. Tony Robbins says that every human has six basic needs that drive our behavior: Certainty, Uncertainty, Significance, Love and Connection, Growth, and Contribution. Tony says, "We all have the same six needs, but how we value those needs and in what order, determines the direction of our life."[2] We usually have two that are the strongest for us, and I believe many artists feel pulled to Significance.

Part of being an artist is about feeling significant. It is a driving force to what we do. (By the way, this isn't a bad thing. It's a basic human need.) If one of these needs (especially one of our top two) isn't being met, we feel out of control or out of balance. If Significance is one of your top two (I'm pretty sure it's one of mine, so I'm right there with you, friend!), it's helpful to be aware of how that cup is being filled. When your family disapproves of your dream pursuit, it might shake your need for significance. If it feels like your dreams don't matter, it might feel like you don't matter. And holy crap that will be the Kryptonite to your significance.

So what do you do when your Kryptonite is activated and you no longer feel significant? The great thing about these human needs is that there are endless ways to fulfill them. If you're not feeling significant within your own family, where else can you feel significant? How else can you feel like you matter? Do you have a spouse or partner? Kids? A friend that you're helping? Bringing value to another person is a great way to feel significant. And as you fill that cup, the emptiness with your family won't be as devastating.

While we're here...I may not personally know you, but I can tell you, without a doubt, you matter. Right now. You are significant to me. I mean, oh my gosh, you're reading my book that I worked on for over a year! You! You're soaking it up and making MY dream come true. You matter to me. A lot. (In case you needed a reminder.)

Now let's chat about Identity. The work I've been doing in this area has been blowing my mind. This would be a great place to insert the <mind-blown emoji>. In Chapters 2 and 3 we essentially talked about shifting your identity to that of a High Achiever. You went through the exercise of evaluating your specific fears that are making up your current identity, and then changed the story to create your new identity. It makes sense, right? Creating a new set of beliefs that support the new direction you want.

Well, the truth is, our identity goes so much deeper than our doubts and fears. Our identity is made up of memorized behaviors, reactions, thoughts, and beliefs. And much of that memorized information comes from our family, our background, and the way in which we grew up.

For example, growing up, I was the artist in the family. My sister was good at sports and numbers, and I was good at art. Once, in high school, my sister and I took the same accounting class (at different times), and I had to drop it because I was failing. My sister got an A in that class. The dynamics and conversations created this identity within me.

Fast forward to my 30s when I decided to start my own business. I wanted to succeed and had big financial goals. But how on earth was I going to do that? I was the artist. I wasn't good at math and accounting. My Dad still makes fun of me because I use my fingers to count. I'm sorry, I'm a visual learner, I need to SEE things!! Needless to say, I really struggled in the beginning to believe I could do this. Because building a business on my own that is financially successful requires qualities that I don't possess (or so I thought, because of this past identity). This was the first time I realized my old identity was sabotaging my dreams.

That awareness changed everything. I decided to change that story. I decided that I was absolutely capable of growing a business and dealing with numbers. I read books. I listened to podcasts. I was even interviewed on a podcast (it's so embarrassing, please don't search for the episode)! And I did it. I created a successful business. I built a business that brought in 6-figures annually. *Me.* The Artist.

I had to change my identity. I had to be a new person. Only, it's not that new. It's just another version of me that isn't tied down by limitations and believes in my infinite potential.

Dr. Joe Dispenza says that our *personal reality* is created by our *personality.*[3] My story is a perfect example of this. Initially, my reality was a failing business because my personality was not good at math. Dr. Dispenza says in order to change our personal reality, we need to change our personality. Which is exactly what I did. I changed my personality to someone who is resourceful and good at learning math and any other subject that will help me succeed. And that created a new reality for myself with a successful business.

What is your identity within your family? What behaviors and thoughts did you grow up with that have impacted who you are today? This role we play or the identity we embody can impact our relationship with our family as we pursue our dreams. I had a lot of money saved from the TV shows I worked on and I decided to invest that money into my business. But I didn't tell my Dad about it until after the business was successful. Because he would have had a heart attack. It's not how my Dad would have used the money, so it would have been hard for him to understand and support my decision. Just like we have our own identity that is built from our upbringing, so do our parents. They have their own behaviors, thoughts, and beliefs that were born from the way in which they grew up. As we become adults and pursue our own endeavors, it may clash with our parents' beliefs. This awareness can provide compassion for them, rather than devastation.

On the surface, an easy solution for lack of support in your vision is to be selective with whom you share it. Remember, it's that newborn baby that needs to be protected. You can disengage from conversations that bring anxiety to your dream. But it's more helpful in the long run if you go deeper. Heal your insecurities. Seek other places to feel significant. Let go of old limiting identities. And believe in your dream so deeply that your confidence becomes contagious.

# *Six*

# SHOW ME THE MONEY

S peaking of identity....

How many artists identify as "starving"? Those two words have been synonymous for as long as I can remember. So I couldn't write this book without addressing it because I'm here to change old paradigms for you.

One day, a client showed me a social media account that had "broke actress" in their handle. This person was labeling their identity, declaring themselves broke, and creating an entire account around this topic. That's a lot of dedication to the broke identity. I understand that perhaps they wanted to relate to so many struggling artists and bring humor and lightness to an otherwise heavy situation. But what they may not realize, is that they are speaking this identity into existence.

They are committing to the struggle, and bringing tons of followers with them.

Even if you don't have a social media handle with the word "broke" in it, there's a good chance you're also clinging to a "starving" identity. You've been fed the story for so long that artists are usually waiting tables and struggling financially, that even if you don't want that story to be true for you, you've unconsciously decided that it's your destiny because you've chosen to be an artist.

There is so much I want to say about this because, holy crap, what a bunch of baloney! Starting with: why on earth would the Universe *want* you to struggle? I think there is a common belief that we can't "have our cake and eat it, too," so it's hard to believe that we can pursue our dreams and be wealthy. It seems like we have to pick one or the other. And even though there are celebrities making millions of dollars per project, therefore showing that it's totally possible to have both, we associate those celebrities with the rare, "oh that hardly ever happens, so it won't be happening for me." Ba-loney. P.S. Am I showing my age by using that word? I can't stop saying it. Baloney!

But, if you haven't figured it out by now, this book's purpose is to create celebrities. I'm not here, typing away 50,000+ words so you can have a mediocre career. Hell. No. I'm here for the big stuff. The grand, life changing stuff. The stuff you feel you're *meant for*. See what I did there? This book is teaching you how to be a High Achiever. I want you to be the celebrity making $20 million dollars a movie (or whatever your dream's version of that is). You are here to have your cake and eat it too, and it's going to be the most delicious cake you've ever eaten in your life! (Plus, no calories!)

In order for that to happen, we've got to talk about how money plays a role in your identity. Because here's the truth, it's nearly impossible to pursue a dream without money. Money is a resource. It's a tool. It's a value exchange. And as you'll recall from Pillar #9, it's essential to building a business (and your dream is a business). But we attach so many deeper stories to money that it becomes really easy to use money as an excuse not to pursue your dream at all. If you identify as broke or poor, you're always going to say "No," to investing in your dream. You're always going to see it as an obstacle to do the things that will help you move forward. And you might be like, "But Erica, I'm not just identifying as broke, I really am broke. Check my bank account! I can't afford shit!" Oh trust me. I've been there, so I know that story well. But here's the difference from not having a ton of money in your bank account to deeply connecting to broke as your identity: When it's not part of your identity, it's simply a current circumstance. When you believe that your success is inevitable and that the Universe is always supporting you, you find a way to invest in the things you need. You get *resourceful*. You ask for help. You take out a loan. You use credit. You sell a bunch of old toys on ebay. Seeing your current circumstance as **temporary**, changes the way you approach investing in your dream. That word right there is the difference—temporary. When you don't identify as broke, you see your lower bank account as temporary. When you identify as broke, you see it as permanent; a dead-end situation.

Your identity is part of you. It's who you are. Your bank account is not who you are. Detaching the two will change your life. Remember those pillars that talked about abundance and always believing in solutions? They apply here, too. Just like that FedEx logo example, if you identify as broke, you'll never see solutions. And I can't stress enough, you need those solution-goggles to make this dream come true. You need to believe that everything is working out for you. You need to believe that the Universe is supporting you. You need to believe that you can absolutely do this, no matter what obstacle pops up in front of you.

I know that artists are often struggling financially. But guess what? That's *a* story, not *your* story. I mean, think about how ridiculous it is to believe such a blanket statement that ALL artists struggle. It's an individual thing. Maybe "most people" struggle. But you're not here to be most people. You're here to be the best, highest version of yourself. You're here to be the High Achiever. So it's time you let go of that story. F#&k that story. It's not yours. You're not going to identify with it. Your story is going to be different, starting now.

I want you to separate your bank account from your identity. You can be wealthy in your identity and have your bank account showing something different. Because your inner being never changes. It's constant. Your inner being can be wealthy, no matter what. It's a state of mind, rather than a current circumstance. And when you make *that* your identity, your bank account will be sure to follow.

So let's do an exercise. Right now, I want you to sit for a moment, close your eyes, and decide that your new identity is wealthy. How does it feel? How do you feel? How do you feel when you're wealthy? How does it impact your day-to-day? Maybe you feel calm. You no longer feel anxious. You pay your bills with ease. Your confidence returns. Take a few minutes and really let this sink in. You are wealthy. It's part of your identity.

Once you open your eyes, I want you to make a list of physical proof that you're wealthy. Look around: do you have a roof over your head? Do you have food to eat? Do you have a comfy bed? Do you have Netflix and Hulu? Do you have a fancy schmancy computer (the kind that gives you access to the internet and other programs you need)? Do you have clothes to wear? These may seem like essentials and nothing "wealthy," but remember, **wealthy is a state of mind.** If you feel wealth, you'll look around and see all the amazing things you have. If you feel broke, you'll look around and see all the amazing things you *don't* have.

Changing your identity is that simple. Well, it can be. There are tons of books you can read that dive deep into wealth consciousness and money mindset (two of my favorites are *Secrets of the Millionaire Mind* by T. Harv Eker and *You Are A Badass At Making Money* by Jen Sincero), but for now, shifting into a wealthy identity is going to be a game changer. Oh, and please don't make the mistake I did when I started learning this. I'll never forget, many years ago, having an argument over Facebook comments with my coach about how broke I was, "You don't understand, I can't even afford a haircut right now. I'm really freaking broke!!" My coach kept telling me that I was abundant and I could afford whatever I wanted, and the more she said it, the more I wanted to scream. I wanted to show her screenshots from my bank account. I wanted to shake her and be like, "HELLO??! ARE YOU KIDDING ME? DON'T YOU GET IT?!"

What I didn't realize at the time, is that I was fighting for my limitations. We tend to do that. We fight so hard to prove our limitations. We fight to show people that we really are struggling. And in that process, we block out any potential solutions or changes. Because when we fight for our limitations, we're declaring them to be permanent, rather than temporary. We're attaching them to our identity. Instead of choosing something different, we're choosing to stay where we are.

In that moment, I could have said, "OK, currently, my bank account doesn't have enough for a haircut at my fancy Los Angeles hair salon.

But this is temporary and I'm going to stop focusing on it. Instead, I'm going to connect to my inner wealth and believe there are endless possibilities of how I can get a haircut. I could go to a cheaper place. I could set the intention to create the money. I could ask my parents for help. I could cut my hair myself. I could focus on the wealth around me and tell stories about how wealthy I am, and see what comes to me in the next few days. I can easily manifest $50. I am wealthy and money is always flowing to me!" That's what you see when you don't identify as broke.

Just like believing your dream is possible will open you up to possibilities, so will believing you have all the money you need. This is a powerful concept because this small shift can be the difference of a fulfilling career and one that never gets off the ground. It's so easy to get stuck in the broke mindset and never feel able to invest in your dreams. Notice a word I said there, *invest*. Investing is great because there is usually a return on investment (or if you're really into business-speak, ROI). If you bought a slice of pizza for $3 and then ate it, you're not going to get those $3 back (a return on that investment). It's just a good ol' *cost*. But with your dream, if you invest in headshots for $500 and those headshots then help you book a role that pays you $1,000, you've just doubled your investment. When you identify as a starving artist, you don't even see the possibility of making more money from the money you spend. You just see all money as a cost -- money that you spend and never see again.

Guess what else stops you from investing (and getting a return)? Not believing you'll succeed. I hope you paid attention to those 10 pillars in Chapter 3 because, man, I'm really whipping them out here! Remember Pillar #7? Your success is inevitable. Pillar #7 says you must believe that your success WILL happen, end of story. People who don't have a strong belief in themselves and their potential to succeed don't believe they'll get a return on their investment because they believe they're going to fail. They don't believe they'll book that $1,000 job. So why spend money when it's never coming back?

See how this trickles down? That's why this first section is so important. It impacts EVERYTHING you do (or don't do). You have to believe in yourself. You have to invest in yourself. You have to believe you'll win, otherwise you'll never try.

Once you can get into your wealthy state of mind -- are you there? I'll wait. Once you're there, money is just about math. Simple math like adding and subtracting (Yes, Dad, the kind I use my fingers to count). You have money come in, and you have money go out. The difference between the two is simple math. If you're already a budgeting wizard, you can skip this paragraph, but I've found that many artists are so tied to their "starving artist" story that they don't even look at the math. They spend money without really knowing how much they're spending, and then they blame all of their money problems on being broke. (Spoiler alert: this totally used to be me, so when I say "they," I'm lumping in past Erica). Knowing your numbers is powerful, and to be honest, it should be something you automatically do. When you feel broke, you should know EXACTLY how much you're spending and EXACTLY how much you're bringing in each month. I'm not here to tell you to stop buying lattes, I'm just telling you to be aware of the lattes you buy. Before you complain that you can't afford something, take a look at your numbers. You might be surprised at what you can afford. When you have overflow, you won't have to count every cent that you spend. But until then, educate yourself on your numbers.

I used to be terrified to look at my bank account because I was mortified to see how little was in there. So I just wouldn't look. Which fed into the problem because I wasn't fully conscious of the amount of money coming in and going out. I know there is a school of thought in my favorite woo-woo manifestation world that essentially says don't look at your bank account if it's negatively affecting your energy, so I listened to that for a while and if I'm really being honest, used it to justify me not looking. "See! These gurus say I don't have to look!" It might work for some people, but for me, it turned out to be a bandaid. It wasn't a deeper solution. Abraham Hicks always says that if you don't like your current circumstances, then don't focus on them. Instead, focus on what you want to create. Which I'm fully here for. But what felt like a better solution for me, was to stop letting my current circumstances trigger me. And they trigger me less when I'm confident in the new circumstances that I'm creating. So I can look at my bank account and not get upset because I know I'm creating a new future for myself. I connect to my wealthy state of mind and can feel grateful for every penny in my account, even if it's just that -- pennies. And using budgeting software like YNAB has been incredibly helpful for me.

I want you to feel empowered in every aspect of your life. With your dreams, with your money, with your relationships. I want you to really get behind the belief that anything is possible and you deserve to have it all. And as I've said before, it starts now. It's all about how you show up in the beginning (and every day after that). If you want to have the resources to invest in your dream, you can be resourceful. You can create money just like you can create opportunities (oh and hey, they're often hand in hand!).

There is always going to be someone who wants to tell you about "reality." And I use quotes around that word because reality is subjective. When someone is reminding you about how expensive things are, and how ridiculous it is that that coach charges so much money to starving artists!, and how little you end up making after taxes and paying people like your agent, they're really just telling you a story about their beliefs and how they live their life (and further committing to the broke identity, because, remember, we get what we focus on). This doesn't have to be your reality. You can focus on abundance instead of scarcity. You can be the person who reminds others, "Isn't it so great that I have the potential to make millions of dollars from my dream? I'm so excited to get there and I love investing in things that help me on that path." Your reality can be different. Because, guess what? We create our own reality.

*Insert make-money-rain gif*

*Seven*

---

# BUY THE
# LOTTERY TICKET

There is an old fable that I've always loved, about a poor man who asked God for help. The man was struggling financially, so every day he would get down on his knees and pray to God, "Please help me win the lottery. I need the money for my family." Day after day, he would make his plea, never seeing a result or receiving an answer. His frustration grew.

"God, are you even listening to me? Please, I need help winning the lottery. We really need the money," he pleaded. Finally, one day the man heard a booming voice answer him. It said, "I'LL HELP YOU IF YOU JUST GO BUY THE LOTTERY TICKET!"

This story has always had a profound impact on me, and the lesson is important for you at this moment. This is the last chapter in the mindset portion of the book. Next, you'll begin the strategy portion where you'll start to take action. It's where the tangible work begins and the resistance kicks in. I can teach you all the things, but it won't make a difference if you don't take action.

There is an author I follow who wrote a book about personal finance. Yesterday, I was scrolling through Twitter and saw this author tweeted a question to his followers. It said: "If you've read my book, where do you still feel stuck?" I scrolled through all of the replies and the author's replies back to the readers. There was an overwhelming common theme: people were starting their questions with, "I haven't finished the book yet but…". They were asking questions that they easily could have learned from the book. Countless people didn't finish the book, not because the book was bad (it's so popular that the author put out a 10th anniversary edition), but most likely because they had resistance to doing the things the book suggested, so they just stopped reading.

I don't want that to happen to you with this book! Many people think that procrastination is a symptom of laziness. But it's not. It always comes down to resistance, and we resist the things we are afraid of. I know you've heard this a million times, but I'm going to say it anyway: everything you want is on the other side of your comfort zone. I love when people see that quote on Instagram and give the hands up emoji like, "Yessssss! Preach! SO true!" and then they go back to watching a Netflix episode instead of sending that email. Intellectually, you know you've got to get outside your comfort zone. But your subconscious is like, "Nah, not today, that's some scary shit and I'm not in the mood. Maybe later!"

Taking action on some of the things in this book might feel scary. Oooo like all the stuff in Chapter 13 (get ready)! But remember everything you've learned so far: Most People don't do the scary stuff. And Most People don't get the great opportunities and the big paychecks. If you want what Most People don't have, you're going to have to do what Most People won't do. Resistance may show up, but you don't have to give in to it. Because you're a freaking star, remember? You're not going to half-ass this dream of yours. You're going to see it through. Because you can't not.

It's helpful to figure out where your resistance is coming from. What are you afraid of? When we know our fears, we can change the story (like you did in Chapter 2). And, by the way, we all have fears. Do you know how scary it was to put this book out into the world? And bear the potential 1-star reviews on Amazon?! But I had to remind myself what was on the other side of my fear: my book making a difference in people's lives and helping them achieve their dreams. I mean, let's be honest, that's so much more important than my fears. I promise it's the same for you. Every time you let the resistance win, you're robbing the world of your gift. How dare you! Can you imagine if Taylor Swift thought, "I don't think I'm good enough. I'm not going to move to Nashville. I'm not going to write songs for the public. I'm not going to put out albums or try to get a record deal." Think of all the people whose lives would be impacted by that decision. You've got some important things to share with us, and we need you! Yes, YOU. When you finish this chapter and move on to the next section, I want you to leave your resistance behind. The impact you're going to make is too important.

There's an exercise called **The 7 Whys** that you can use to figure out what you're afraid of. Even if you think you're super self aware and you know what your fears are, I would still encourage you to try this because it may uncover something you didn't know was there. All you have to do is think of a specific task that you've been procrastinating, and ask yourself "Why?" seven times (ask yourself "Why?" to every answer you give). The answer you get on the 7th why is usually the true answer to the first question. Let me show you an example with a common place actors, writers, and directors feel resistance:

1. Why have you procrastinated submitting to agents?
    *a. Because I don't know what to say in an email.*
2. Why don't you know what to say in an email to agents?
    *a. Because I haven't had that many accomplishments yet in my career.*
3. Why does it matter that you haven't had many accomplishments yet in your career?
    *a. Because an agent wants someone who is experienced and talented.*
4. Why aren't you talented?
    *a. I don't know. Sometimes I think I am, sometimes I don't think I am.*
5. Why do you think sometimes you're not talented?
    *a. When I compare myself to others.*
6. Why do you compare yourself to others?
    *a. Because I might be competing against them and I know I'd lose.*
7. Why would you lose?
    *a. Because I'm not good enough.*

Now go back and read that last answer in relation to Question #1. Why have you procrastinated submitting to agents? *Because I'm not good enough.* Ohhhh. There we go. The truth comes out! Do you see how easy it is to come up with a surface level reason for why we procrastinate, when in reality it's resistance to something? Our mind plays tricks on us and comes up with great excuses, so we usually don't even realize what's really going on. But having this awareness is powerful because it gives us the opportunity to change the story. We can stop using our fear as an excuse to not move forward and instead, embrace the new story we write for ourselves (like, "I'm talented and I'm getting better all the time!"). Because, remember, we create our own reality. You get to live in a reality where you're good enough for an agent...if you choose it.

I'm always fascinated when people don't do the things they should be doing to make their dreams happen. Intellectually, I know it's due to fear. But for me, my fear has never been that debilitating. My desire for my dream has always been greater than my fear. Always. I do experience resistance every now and then, but I'll eventually move past it. Meanwhile, there are countless people who sit in the resistance their whole life and never move forward. In my twelve years in Los Angeles, I've seen many people move here to pursue a Hollywood dream, and then never really go for it. They move their entire life across the country, leaving behind everything that's familiar, and still never fully pursue their dream. They'll get a day job, make some friends, and create a life out here. They might take an acting class or do some low budget work, but they never truly make the leap to where they want to be. If that's you, I'm not insulting you. But I want to light a fire under you and tell you to go for it! Fear can be our greatest enemy. And it all goes back to our subconscious wanting to keep us safe. But playing it safe or small will never produce epic results.

Tony Robbins says that people are motivated by one of two things: pain or pleasure. When you want something, it's either moving towards pleasure or moving away from pain. I think that pain is often the greatest motivator—people don't take action until the pain of their current circumstances becomes too great. For example, when I started my coaching business, I was still working full time in television. For a while, I was able to maintain both. But after my business started growing, it became increasingly difficult. I was working long TV hours on a show and then going home to work on my business at night. Slowly, I started to see that something needed to change. If I really wanted my business to take off, I was going to have to quit my full time TV job. I also had a boss who was incredibly mean to me when he was stressed, giving me extra incentive to leave. But every day that I considered quitting, I would chicken out. Taking that leap to go full time with my business, especially when it hadn't replaced my TV income yet, was terrifying. So I stayed. And I questioned. And I stayed. And I questioned. Until one day when I snapped. My boss had degraded me yet again, and for some reason that felt like the last straw. The pain of staying became too great. So I politely put in my notice and that was it.

When you catch yourself procrastinating on the ideas in this book, do a pain check. One dangerous thing I've noticed is that instead of the pain becoming too great, it actually becomes too comfortable. People actually get comfortable with their painful situations, and they're able to live with it. So it never gets to the point where they feel ready to do something different. That's when you need to connect with the pleasure of what you're pursuing. What pleasure is on the other side of taking action? What's out there waiting for you? How much better will it feel when you start succeeding? If you're numb to the pain, aim for pleasure.

To sum up, just go do everything in the rest of this book, okay?! You're not here to live a mediocre version of your dreams. When you feel meant for something, it's bigger than a goal you set. It's bigger than a cool thing you do some time. **It's your purpose.** It's deep inside of you, all-consuming, and as they say in that classic movie, *It Takes Two* (Starring Mary-Kate and Ashley Olsen, duh!) it's that can't-eat, can't-sleep, reach-for-the-stars, over-the-fence, World Series kind of stuff. And sure, they're talking about love, but being in love with a person and having a meant-for-this dream are not too different from each other. World Series kind of stuff is going to require you to play at a higher level (pun intended). Now's your chance. You can absolutely do this. So, go!

**PART 2**

# Act Like A Star

*Progress always involves risk;*
*you can't steal second base and keep your foot on first.*
FREDERICK B. WILCOX

# Eight

# INSPIRED STRATEGY: THE STRATEGY OF VISIONARIES

A re. You. READY??? (This question is for you but also a little bit for me. Like, holy crap, this is the mecca of all chapters, I can't believe it's time!) As of now, you should feel on freaking FIRE!! You should believe in yourself like you've never believed in yourself before. You should feel more energized to go after your dream, and have a completely new sense of what's possible. (If you're not quite there yet, it's totally okay. The first section of this book is one you should reread time and time again, so go back whenever you need to refuel.)

Now that your Energy is optimal, we're diving into the second step on that Luck formula: Strategy. Ahhhh! I heard music in my head. I feel like I was meant to teach you this very chapter and I'm literally bouncing my leg as I type this. I'm so excited! And not even the Jessie Spano kind of excited—I'm not scared! Just. So. Ready.

Great, now that I've built this up so much, let's do this, shall we?

One of the most important lessons I've learned pursuing a career in Hollywood, is that there is no one way to do anything in this industry. And that is true for all big dreams. There is no one way to achieve your dream. Read that again because people will try to sell you on ways (even friends or peers). But the truth is, you could line up 100 successful people in your field and you would probably hear 100 different stories of how they did it. While that might sound maddening, it's actually quite liberating. Because, holy possibilities!

If there was only one way you could succeed at your dream, it would suck. What would you do if that one way didn't work for you? You'd be devastated and out of ideas. Here, you've got endless possibilities. And I'm going to show you how to find your possibilities. One day, you're going to be interviewed on a talk show, and you're going to share some crazy story about how you landed that amazing next level opportunity, and it's going to be unique to you. People are going to respond like, "Wow! I can't believe that's how it happened! Damn, you got lucky!" And you'll smile with a bit of a smirk and reply, "I didn't get lucky. I got Inspired Strategy." BOOM. Mic drop.

Before we dive into the juiciness of Inspired Strategy (and how it led to this very book you're reading), let's begin with a foundational strategy. This is something I take all of my clients through, and it's a great way to get your basic path. Once you have your foundational strategy, then we're going to sprinkle a little magic on it, but we can't do that until you've got the foundation.

Remember that list you made in Chapter 1? The one that had all of your hopes and dreams on it? It's time to take it out. I want you to pick one dream on there for which we'll create a strategy. This is where your "big" dream becomes tangible. It's no longer going to be this fluffy thing you dream about. Now it's going to be a legitimate goal you pursue. And through these steps, you'll see how tangible it can be.

At the foundation, we want to come up with basic steps you need to take to achieve this dream. Remember my multi-million dollar house story? It felt completely out of reach until I started taking steps. I went to open houses, I spoke to realtors and lenders, I've learned what my income needs to be and how to get there, etc. An out-of-reach "pipe dream" became something I can actually do. So let's figure out what your foundational steps should be. Jack Canfield has a great exercise that I lovingly call WWHH, which stands for What Would Have to Happen? It's a question you can ask to build your dream ladder. We start by working backwards, to figure out the steps you need to take. Start by drawing a rectangle on the top of a piece of paper (see example on next page). Inside that rectangle, write the dream you chose from your list. For an example, I'll go with "Win An Oscar."

Next, we're going to work backwards by asking, "What would have to happen [to win an Oscar]?" We're looking for the very last thing that would happen right before your dream. So, in this example, the very last thing that would have to happen before winning an Oscar would be to be nominated for the Oscar. (We could say there are steps between being nominated and winning, such as marketing and getting the word out so the Academy will vote for you, but we're looking for the broader strokes here.) So I'd write "Be nominated" in the second rectangle below the Oscar. Then we'd ask the question again: "What would have to happen [to be nominated]?" What's the very last thing that would have to happen in order to get to this step? For this example, I'd say: Work on an Oscar-worthy film.

We keep asking this question and working our way down the ladder. As you'll see in the example, you may have more than one item for each step, and in that case you can split the ladder level into two or three boxes. What you'll notice, is that we are reverse engineering your dream. We're working backwards to figure out what needs to happen. When you take luck out of the equation, every success can be reverse engineered. I want you to remember that. Every success can be reverse engineered.

If you're having trouble filling in your ladder and you're not sure what your steps are, ask someone. Google it. Research. Remember: you are solution-oriented. It's easy to say, "I don't know" and then give up. Solutions are all around you, and it's as simple as a Google search. Once you have your ladder, I want you to take a look at it and repeat a 3-year old from one of my favorite tweets (by @jendziura): "That's just 4 things." Okay, maybe my example is about 6 things, but the point is, you are only a few steps away from that dream you thought was so out of reach! That's worth doing a little dance. *dance break*

So now you've got this foundational strategy. These are the main steps that you can work towards. But remember when I said there is no one-way to achieve your dream? That's because it's going to take magic in between these steps. And your magic may look very different from someone else's. With my example, how you get the agent, or how you make the connections, or how you get noticed...have a million different ways they could play out. Oh, and the fun part: you could even skip steps! My cousin directed a movie that received four Oscar nominations and one of them was for Best Actress for the leading girl who was only 9 years old at the time of nomination. She was pulled from obscurity in Louisiana, had never acted professionally before, booked the film, and was nominated for an Oscar. Like, holy magic! Now, you could go, "Ohh okay, great. I'll move to Louisiana and just live my life, hoping that a film comes to town looking for me." But that's just crazy pants. That was Quvenzhané Wallis' story. Not yours. When we try to replicate other people's magic, it takes us out of the running for our own. So while we can reverse engineer the basic steps, the magic has to be unique to us.

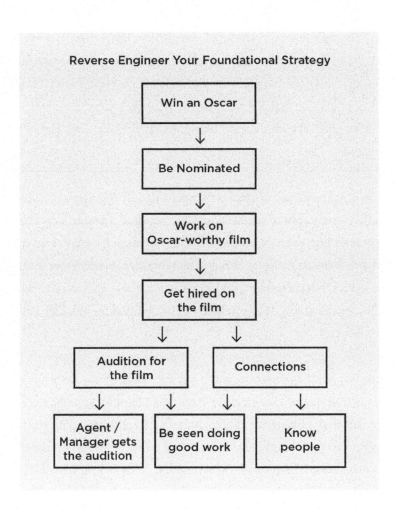

## INSPIRED STRATEGY

Inspired Strategy started as a fun side exercise I did with my clients. I was inspired by the book The Alchemist, where a boy sets out to find treasure, and along the way hits many obstacles. But each obstacle ended up leading to his next step, just like a scavenger hunt, and it became evident that each obstacle was there on purpose. I loved this idea so much that I created a "Scavenger Hunt" for my clients. I encouraged them to record every obstacle and note where it led them next. I thought this would be a fun way for my clients to get out of their heads when they hit obstacles, and instead of feeling discouraged, feel excited about where it's going to lead. My clients would get 10 points for every obstacle that led to something, so they were actually being rewarded when they hit a wall. Imagine that! I know, I thought I was very clever.

Actually, it wasn't just obstacles they recorded. It was also synchronicities (like crazy coincidences), and inspired ideas. I wanted my clients to pay attention to these other two things because they also lead us to the best places. It's easy to shrug off a random idea we get or a weird coincidence, but then we might be missing our next clue. So this whole game was essentially seeing where you are guided to, just like a scavenger hunt.

Then, last year, I started to really pay attention to my own clues. It happened in one of those divine ways that's hard to describe because there isn't a super tangible explanation. But it all started with the idea to write this book. Actually, it happened a few moments before that, and if this were a script I would totally CUT TO FLASHBACK.

On October 1st, my friend asked if I wanted to join her volunteering at Gabby Bernstein's book launch event. It wasn't something I'd normally do, and I had only read one of Gabby's books. But I was creatively struggling most of the year, feeling lost and confused about what I wanted to do next in my life, and the thought of doing something different felt refreshing. Something told me to say yes.

So when the day of the event arrived, I drove over to the Wilshire Ebell Theater. There were double doors at the entrance, and as I made my way through them, I saw volunteers frantically opening boxes of books and journals and setting them up on tables. I jumped in and helped open boxes.

Shortly after, one of the doors burst open, and like a model off the runway, Gabby Bernstein entered the theater. It felt like one of those moments in a movie where they slow down the speed and show Gabby walking in slow motion, with a fan blowing her hair behind her—the star had arrived.

And in that moment, my world slowed down, too. As I stood up and watched Gabby check in with her event coordinator and make her way to the green room backstage, my heart started beating out of my chest and a voice spoke to me. "I want that," the voice said. It came from within and completely threw me. My heart was glowing and I felt a sense of peace wash over me. "I want that," the voice repeated.

I didn't even know what "that" really was. But something in that moment felt connected. Something told me, this is it. The entire year I had tried to think my way to my next thing. I questioned what I was doing with my life and felt disconnected from everything I tried. I brainstormed, I took courses, I worked with coaches. I desperately sought the answer all year. And then, in one moment, I felt my way to the answer. It didn't come about from a brainstormed list. It didn't come from talking it out. It wasn't something I finally found. It was something I received.

When I watched Gabby speak on stage about her latest book and inspire over a thousand people, including a handful of Hollywood celebrities, the voice kept calling, "I want that." The "that" became clearer, and through a series of similar moments throughout the next few months, I felt called to write this book and embark on a speaking career. It was the first time in a long time I felt meant for something. It felt bigger than me. It wasn't a goal I had to strategize, it was a message I had to share and a path I had received.

Over the next few months, I felt guided to every step. It felt like the Universe was giving me directions and I was simply following them. I kept receiving the directions through inspired ideas that never felt like they were coming from my intellectual brain. It felt like it was coming from a divine place, leading me where I needed to go. It had been so long since I had a new dream, that I forgot what this felt like. And I think, for the first time, I fully trusted the guidance like I never had before, making every step completely effortless. I had no fears, I had no doubts. I didn't even see obstacles when they showed up because it all felt perfect. It felt like I was floating on a cloud, and then slowly, the dreaminess of it started to wear off.

I decided that was the honeymoon period. And oh, was it glorious. When a dream is so new and exciting that there is no resistance at all. I can't even remember the last time I felt that way. I mean, no resistance? What kind of utopia was I living in?! I hadn't been rejected yet or had to work hard at the process. I remember talking to my astrologer (yes, of course I have one of those) and she warned me, "This is so great! You want to write this book! It's going to be great. But it's going to be a process. There's going to be work involved." I didn't even believe her. LOL. So cute, Erica. Definitely honeymooning with my book. But this was truly a wonderful gift because it led me to Inspired Strategy. It showed me how to use my intuitive guidance to get me from one foundational ladder step to the next. And the synchronicities along the way blew my mind. I know they were put there to help me maintain the faith and show me how magical this Universe really is.

About two weeks before I volunteered at Gabby's event, I was inspired to research celebrities I wanted to work with. I was ready to up my coaching game, and felt excited to work with people doing positive work in the world. I made a list and sent it to my assistant. We both continued to add names over the next few days of people who felt like a good match to the work I do. Then, two weeks later, while I was working Gabby's event, one of the celebrities from that list walked by me and said, "Hello!" My mouth dropped! (On the inside, of course.) I couldn't believe it. I had no idea she would be at this event. It felt like a wink from the Universe saying, "Yes, Erica, go in this direction! We've got this!"

One of the other celebrities on my list has a production company. They're putting out projects with positive messages and feel totally in line with what I do. I thought it would be great to meet with this company and collaborate in some way. In December, I did an intimate live event at Warner Bros. It was the first time I taught Inspired Strategy, and I shared a picture of this particular celebrity, explaining how I felt guided to work with this person. That night, after the event, I received an email from one of the attendees saying, "Erica, I really loved the event! By the way, I'm friends with that celebrity. I've worked with him and he's really great. Do you want me to see if I can introduce you?" Holy crap! I mean, of course, right? That attendee booked a lunch with this celebrity several months later when he was free, and talked about me. The celeb said he had too much on his plate right now but it would be great if I could be introduced to his partner (Co-founder of the production company). I was ecstatic to hear this news, and we tried to set up a meeting with the co-founder. But the timing wasn't right, as he had just had a baby with his wife.

A month or two passed and we reached out again, this time with no answer. I let it go and trusted that it would happen whenever it was supposed to happen. Then, one day, I was on Facebook and a post popped up from someone in my college alumni group. He said he worked for the production company! I couldn't believe this. Yet another connection to this company! Immediately, I posted and let him know I was waiting to hear back from the co-founder. The next thing I knew, the college guy and I were hopping on a video chat. It was a great conversation, and that led to an official meeting with the co-founder. We spoke about potential collaborations and ways we could help each other. Just six months after I set the intention, the meeting came to be. What's crazy is that the college guy didn't even work for the company six months ago. This was a new job he had recently started. Someone else might call this luck, but I know I co-created it with the Universe.

Do you see how that story is not formulaic? Connections sort of fell into my lap. I followed my inspired ideas and let the Universe guide me. From a tangible standpoint, you could say I used my current connections to reach out to a new connection. But it's so much more fun than that over-simplified version. This is Inspired Strategy.

Now that you have your foundational ladder, let yourself be guided to the spaces in between. Our intuition is the only "lucky break" we'll ever need. It's wiser than any class or course. The answers we seek are often inside ourselves, and when we quiet the outside noise and listen internally, we're always led to where we need to be. You'll also find that when you're in your Star Power, ideas will flow to you. You'll feel inspired more often than not and things seem to just *happen*. This doesn't mean we abandon the foundation (I mean, hello, I have 13 more chapters of actions you can take!), it just means we have ways to make the foundation work for us.

To create your own Inspired Strategy, start with the four modes: Inspired Ideas, Obstacles, Coincidences, Connection. I've already mentioned these before, but let's break them down so you know how to make them work for you: Inspired Ideas are the ideas that come to you intuitively. You get them in the shower, while driving, in conversation, exercising, etc. For example, one morning I felt inspired to record a motivational speech set to music like the ones I listen to at the gym. I recorded it and designed artwork to go with it for Apple Music, and when I saw the artwork finished, I heard a voice tell me this was the cover for my book. (Check the cover to see!)

Obstacles are when you get a "No" or hit a wall. They are a chance to pivot, and lead somewhere else. For example, when I wasn't brought back to that long-running TV show, and then booked Chasing Life, my most enjoyable TV experience. When one door closes, another one is surely around the corner. Coincidences are those too-crazy-to-be-a-coincidence moments where the Universe is trying to get your attention. Like seeing the celebrity from my list show up at Gabby's event. And lastly, Connection is when you have an emotional connection or reaction to something you see or hear, just like I did at Gabby's event. I knew it was a strategy I had to pay attention to because I felt it deeply in my heart. Once, I even spent an entire day crying (I know, very sexy!) when an idea came. It impacted me that much, and I knew

I had to pay attention.

Through these four ways, you'll be led to ideas that will take you from one step on your ladder to the next. Hell, it may even have you skip a rung! In order for your Inspired Strategy to powerfully move you up, your inspired ideas should include risk. Remember that third part of the luck formula? Risk is an important piece of the puzzle and you'll likely be led to what risks you should take. Your ideas should also feel aligned. They may be a little scary because they're new or outside your comfort zone, but they should make you excited. And one of the most important parts: your ideas must stem from your belief that what you want is possible. I can't say that enough (you may be sick of hearing this, but I can't stop!). If you're feeling limited in your possibilities, your inspired ideas will also be limited. Oh, and it's okay if no one else is doing your idea. That's kind of the point, right? For them to be yours. It doesn't mean you have to reinvent the wheel, but your ideas should lead you on your own unique path.

By the way, inspired ideas that come from your intuition are not the same as ideas that come from your ego. Here's how you can tell the difference: ideas that come from your ego are usually fear-based or focused on validation. They are safe. And they may be leading you toward an "easier" approach (because your ego doesn't believe that you can actually get the big dream you want). On the other side, ideas from your intuition will surprise and excite you. It will feel right in your body. And most likely, it will be outside your comfort zone.

When you're a visionary, the path appears. You're meant for this, so of course the path will reveal itself. You just have to be open to it looking a little different than everyone else's. Since I started using Inspired Strategy, I recorded all four modes whenever they happened. I documented them in categories and labeled them: Guided Idea, Synchro-nicity, Opportunity. The Guided Ideas came to me through one of the four modes. Technically, synchronicity is a mode here, but I also documented them as proof that my plan is working and I'm on the right path. When I followed these ideas and synchronicities, opportunities began to happen. In just a single month (November, 2019), I had seven inspired ideas come to me that I acted on, five synchronicities to back up those ideas, and two major opportunities fell into my lap. This is how I make my foundational strategy work. This is how I find my way.

Think of it like this: you and your intuition are a team. You've got the foundation covered—that's all logical. Those steps are created from data-driven information. Your intuition, on the other hand, will cover everything else. Your intuition will lead you to your data-driven steps. It will give you ideas, lead you to connections, and guide you to places. If your foundational ladder is the head in this equation, your intuition is the heart. Like scavenger hunt clues being whispered in your ear, your intuition tells you where to turn. When you combine that with the tangible strategy, you'll never lose. Create your own yellow-brick-road, because you've always had the power, my dear.

*Nine*

# THE ONLY ACTIONS
# THAT MATTER

've always struggled with acne growing up and it's been one of my biggest insecurities. When I moved to LA, it seemed to get worse because apparently the water here is very different (every pizza chef reinforces this, that's why the dough is better on the east coast). So I yelped my way to a facialist who worked out of her home in a neighborhood not too far from mine. She was a kind woman with a Russian accent and even though I was kind of scared for whatever painful treatment she was about to perform, I got the feeling she knew what she was doing. (Plus, all those Yelp reviews!)

It did hurt a bit, but I survived, and as I was gathering my things to leave, she said something that stuck with me for almost a decade.

"What products do you use to fight acne?" she inquired. It was leading to a sales pitch, but trust me, the lesson was worth it...

She pressed on, "What do you use to clean your face to fight acne?"

I answered confidently, "Oh, I use Cetaphil. It says right on the bottle that it's a gentle cleanser!" Meaning, safe for sensitive skin like mine.

"That's great," she replied "But what do you use to fight acne?" It took the repetition of her question for me to finally hear what she was saying, and a light bulb went off over my head.

OH. MY. GOSH. I was using a gentle cleanser. It wasn't bad. But it also wasn't going to get me real results. Because it didn't actually do the thing I needed. I bought her homemade products and took home a lesson that I lovingly pushed on all of my clients for years to come:

Where in your life are you using a gentle cleanser instead of a face wash that fights acne? This is what I call Soft Actions versus Hard Actions. Guess which ones are the only actions that matter?

**SOFT ACTIONS V. HARD ACTIONS**

Soft actions are the gentle cleanser for your dream. They are the actions you take that are great, but they don't actually lead you directly to a result. For example, taking a class. It's not bad to take a class. In fact, you should probably brush up on your craft so you can be good at what you do. But when it comes to actions, taking a class isn't going to get you a job. It might prepare you for the job, but it won't open the door. The gentle cleanser, if you will.

Hard actions, on the other hand, are the actions that lead directly to a result. Like interviewing for a job. Auditioning. Connecting to someone who can help you. Advertising. Making an ask. The acne-fighters!

Even though Hard actions could lead to a "No," it's still a hell of a lot closer to getting a "Yes," than taking a class.

What I've found, is that if we took an inventory of most people's actions, it would be 90% soft, 10% hard. (I know, I know, it's almost impossible not to make a sexual joke. Let's be grownups for a minute, k?!) Some people are closer to 0% when it comes to hard actions. If we dive back into that refreshing High Achiever's pool, we'll find the opposite: they're more like 90% hard, 10% soft. High Achievers focus on the actions that lead to results. It doesn't mean that they don't do things like take a class. It just means that they're also spending a majority of their time making the ask. In business, it's called money-making activities. In art, it's called putting yourself out there (which, hey! often leads to money-making activities, because, oh right, your art is a business, too).

The discrepancy is obvious: hard actions are outside your comfort zone. So of course they're scarier. People shy away from scary. They like safe. They like comfortable. And man, is that class comfortable. It makes you feel good because you can fail and succeed in a safe environment. But the potential of failing in the real world is just too much for some people to take. Obviously, not you. I mean, you've got your Star Power. But maybe the old you...

It's so easy to get stuck in researching and experimenting and sitting in a cave creating your art. And you should be doing those things. But if that's all you do, the dream will never happen. If I kept using that gentle cleanser and never switched to an acne fighting face wash, I would never get the clearer skin I desired. The gentle cleanser isn't bad. But it's also not results-oriented. Now is the time to take inventory of your actions. Take a look back at your Reverse Engineer ladder. None of those steps are going to happen by soft actions alone. Soft actions might prepare you for those steps. But it's the hard actions that will actually lead you there.

Oh, and let's chat about being busy. "Busy" is soft actions disguised as hard actions. Artists love to feel busy. Especially in a dream pursuit where it feels like they have no control. When you're busy, it feels like you have your control back. It feels like you're doing something. It feels like you're productive. When you're busy, you feel like you're perceived as successful. People must think you're doing something right because, man, you're so busy all the time! But the truth is, being busy is a way we distract ourselves from whatever we don't want to face. If you feel like you're not succeeding, being busy is a great way to take your mind off of that painful realization.

Sometimes (okay, maybe more often than sometimes), as I coach, I teach the thing I need to hear most. So I'll be vulnerable (i.e. embarrassed for a minute) and give you a great example of how being busy distracts us from the hard actions: right now, as I write these pages, I could be submitting to agents and publishers to help get this book out into the world. And I have done that. But right now, writing the book is so comfy and I'm enjoying being in this safe little bubble. But, like, Erica, get your shit together. I need to submit to publishers so that hopefully you're reading these words from a published book! Writing is a soft action. It's something I need to do, obviously. But just writing this book won't get it published. See where I'm going? I can pretend to be sooo busy writing these pages, but that doesn't mean I'm actually closer to getting this book published. People might perceive me to be closer. But I won't be closer until I send out more proposals. Umm... brb while I go eat my own words.

Many of my private clients would suddenly feel like they had so much more free time after working with me because we'd only focus on the actions that matter, and let go of the busy work. If you're busy with soft actions, you'll never really break free of being busy with soft actions. Especially if you have a day job to support your dream. If you're working 40 hours a week with a day job, that means you only have a few hours every day (or even every week) to work on your dream. So let's say you have five hours a week outside of your day job (I mean, you could sleep less, but I never like that option because I need 8 hours), and you spend three of those five hours in class, and the other two hours doing homework for that class. After a month, you'll have spent 20 hours on class, and 0 hours on the actions that will move you closer to your dream. Imagine if, instead, you spent those 20 hours a month on interviewing, auditioning, sending cold emails, and making an ask. Can you imagine how much closer you'd be to your dream after a month?

Aim for 90/10. Or even 80/20. The majority of your time should be spent on hard actions, i.e. putting yourself out there. I know it's scary, but you've got this. Access your inner Star Power and start making that ask. Here are a list of examples I see in Hollywood for both soft and hard actions:

**Soft:**
- Taking a class
- Researching
- Writing
- Practicing your craft
- Watching TV shows/films
- Refining your marketing materials
- Meditating
- Journaling
- Writer's groups

- Creating your own content (this can fall into both categories, depending how you use it...you can easily use it as a thing to feel busy and in control and as a way to avoid taking risks)

**Hard:**
- Auditioning
- Interviewing
- Submitting to agents or managers
- Making an ask
- Making connections for the sole purpose of moving forward
- Asking for a referral
- Asking for distribution for your project
- Selling your project or script
- Pitching
- Marketing/Advertising
- Submitting to festivals
- Submitting to competitions
- Cold emailing
- Creating your own content (with the purpose of it leading somewhere specific like festivals, distribution, selling, representation, etc.)

You'll notice that the soft actions are all great actions. You should be doing them on your journey to your dream. But imagine if you only did them. You're not going to journal your way to an interview. You might journal your way to an inspired idea or newly found confidence that leads to an action that leads to an interview. But there's going to be a hard action in between there, connecting the dots.

Hard actions will support the strategy you build from your foundational ladder and fill in the Risk in the Luck formula. Remember, opportunities won't come without risk. You have to put yourself out there. You have to give people a chance to say "Yes" to you. Embrace your Star Power. Engage in a star-powered strategy. Take those star-powered risks. And doors will inevitably open. The dream is yours when you decide to go for it.

# *Ten*

# MORE DOORS!

M y mom always tells me the story about the time I was a toddler and she would take me along as she ran errands. There was a strip mall a few minutes away from where we lived, and as we walked by each store, I would say, "More doors! More doors!" It's as if the toddler in me was speaking metaphorically for opportunities. I mean, probably not, but let's pretend!

So much of your dream is dependent upon opportunities, therefore, we want to create as many as possible. And since an opportunity is simply a door opening, we want to knock on as many doors as possible. Also, side note: can we just take a minute to feel some gratitude for how easy it is to knock on doors these days? Decades ago, our parents had to literally knock on doors. You know that's where the phrase comes from, right?! Before cold calling and cold emailing, there was cold door knocking. Talk about scary. Instead of someone deleting your email, they would literally slam a door in your face. Now, thanks to the invention of the internet, "knocking on doors" is so much easier, less time consuming, and a hell of a lot less scary. But I digress...

Before we get into this, let's define what a "door" is. For me, knocking on a door is the equivalent of making an ask. This ask can take on many forms, like an interview or audition (where you're essentially asking for a job), or something like sending a cold email, where you make an ask to someone you don't know. This can also include submissions, such as submitting to a competition or festival, or submitting to an agent. Everything that could be considered knocking on a literal door if we got in our Delorean and traveled back in time.

Your dream is going to require lots of knocking. You'll need people to hire you or buy from you or give you an opportunity. Those opportunities come when you ask for them. There's no getting around it (well, technically the Universe can make things feel like they're falling into your lap, but it's still going to involve you taking action). So here's my ultimate advice on this topic: ask until you get your "Yes." I've found that most people give up asking much too soon. They knock on 20 doors and feel discouraged and exhausted, and take it as a sign that maybe they're just not meant for this. But OH YEAH. Remember what we said before? You are the only one who gets to decide if you're meant for this. It's not up to fate, it's a decision. Getting 20 rejections is not a sign to give up. It just means you've got to keep knocking if you want this dream.

There are countless people in history who had to knock on a million doors before becoming the success for which we know them. My man Jack Canfield had 144 publishers turn him down for *Chicken Soup For*

*The Soul.* They didn't think it would sell. Then one little publisher in Florida decided to publish it and the book series went on to sell 110 million copies, with the worldwide retail sales of branded products exceeding $2 billion.[4] Barbara Streisand was rejected 40 times for roles in her career. Babs! When I broke into Hollywood, I cold emailed about 150 people before Henry helped me. One of my clients cold emailed 250 managers before signing with a top 25 one. Can you imagine if any of us stopped after the 20th rejection?

We have to talk about this because there is a popular concept (that I am totally behind) that essentially contradicts this strategy: the definition of insanity is doing the same thing over and over again and expecting a different result. According to that concept, it's insane to knock on that 145th door and expect to get a different result than you've been getting. In general, I fully believe this concept. But it gets tricky here. There is a fine line between giving up on a door too soon, and deciding that door isn't opening. I think this is nuanced but here is my generalized rule for this: It's not insane to knock on doors until you get a yes. It is insane to pursue the same avenue for years and expect something new to happen. That's why I wanted to define what a "door" is. Because you can essentially knock on a door, and also knock on a path. I'll explain how the two are different but I want to add some nuance to the door:

While I don't believe it's insane to knock on more doors, I have found that it can be insane to knock on doors the exact same way and expect something different. In my experience, the more doors you knock on, the more opportunities you'll get to refine your pitch. You might get helpful feedback along with your rejection, or you might simply grow as an artist and that leads to new ideas. For example, when I was submitting this book to agents and publishers, I tweaked my query letter and proposal many times. Even after I had already submitted to

9 agents, I wrote a completely new overview. When I submitted to the first few agents, I didn't even have a title for the book! So as time went on, I refined my pitch. I didn't ask the same way. I didn't decide that submitting to agents wasn't working, I decided I needed to get better and clearer in my asking.

Avenues, on the other hand, are different. As I've said ad nauseam, there is no one way to make your dream happen. That means, if you try one way for years and aren't seeing results, it's time to try a different way. For example, there are many paths to become a screenwriter for television. You could start on a TV show as a Writer's PA or Writer's Assistant and move your way up into the writer's room. Or you could assist a producer on a TV show and get promoted. Or you could assist a writer who has an overall deal with a studio and get a writer's slot when one of their shows gets picked up. Lauryn Kahn was the assistant to big time movie producer Adam McKay (he was Will Ferrell's producing partner up until 2019), and Adam helped her sell her first script for ONE MILLION DOLLARS! Or you could skip the lower-level jobs altogether and get an agent or manager who helps you get staffed. Or that manager could help you sell your own show that you continue to write on. Oh, and you could also get into a studio's writing program (like ABC) where they often place you on a show. So, if you can count (yes I'm using my fingers, duh), that's seven different ways right there that could lead to being staffed on a show as a writer. We'll call those seven different avenues. What commonly happens, is that a writer will pursue one of those for many years, get stuck, and never try another one. *That's* insanity. People get comfortable in the avenue they choose, and fear trying a new one.

Did you notice that all seven of those ways lead directly to being staffed as a writer? I didn't say, "Or you could work as an extra on TV shows and hope you make connections there that will somehow lead to a writing job." Don't confuse a new avenue with a dream-adjacent one. Our mind likes to trick us and the fear of failure can manifest into indirect paths where the strategy is wishing and hoping, rather than calculated and intentional. It's common to have good intentions and want to try something new, but end up trying something that will rarely lead you to where you want to go. It's under the guise of, "I don't want to be insane! This isn't working, so I should try something else!" but ultimately takes you off course.

It all comes back to believing your success is inevitable. When you believe in that outcome, you'll always choose the most direct path. Even when it's time for a new avenue, you'll be strategic and intentional with your choice. And remember that Luck formula? Sometimes the door isn't opening because of your energy. What are your beliefs behind every action you take? How do you feel when you knock on that door? Are you feeling defeated? Are you feeling discouraged and sad? Are you feeling desperate? That energy can block a door from opening just as much as a poorly laid out strategy. When doors aren't opening, check in with your four luck elements: How is your energy? How is your strategy? Is this a risk? Do you need to tweak your thoughts? Do you need to tweak your pitch? Do you need to tweak your actions? Or is it truly time for a new door?

It will be helpful to decide how you define a path or door not working. People always ask me, "How many emails should I send? 100?" and it's never about the actual quantity. It's about however many it takes to open the door. Only you can put limits there. How many knocks will it take before you decide to give up? There is no formulaic answer here, it has to come from within. Me...I don't ever give up. There is no number I could call out for a sign that I should quit asking. None.

I may adjust my strategy or look for another way in. But I will never stop. My desire is too strong. And I believe that anything is possible if you keep going. So that's what I do, I keep going.

For doors, you can never knock on too many. You can never ask for what you want too many times. There is no number there that says you should stop. Avenues, on the other hand, can certainly have a timeline. If you're pursuing one path for a year or more and not getting any traction, you can try another path. But only you will know when it's time. Your intuition will let you know. But before you switch it up, make sure you've truly exhausted this one. Have you given it your best? Have you done everything in your power? Back to the TV writer example, you could easily work as a Writer's PA for years and never move up and blame it on the path. But did you actually ask? Did you ask more than once? Were you clear and assertive? There are obviously times when you consistently ask and never get the promotion. I've seen that happen in Hollywood many times. But I think it's more common to be timid in your asking (or not ask at all) and then blame it on someone else. If anything, I hope this book empowers you to stand up and ask for what you want. I know there is a fear that if you ask wrong or piss someone off, you'll blow all your chances, but I don't believe your chances are limited. I believe we have *unlimited* chances. And I also believe you were given this dream for a reason. So ask for it! Do I need to remind you again...? You. Are. Meant. For. This. So make that ask.

P.S. Multiple avenues are not the same as multiple interests. As artists or creative people, it's easy to have a million ideas you want to pursue. You might be interested in different mediums, different projects, different businesses. I think that's amazing -- I mean, the fact that our imagination can still have the freedom to run wild, even as an adult, is such a gift. But the problem we run into, is when we try to pursue all of these at once.

*Don't shoot the messenger* People want to throw rocks at me when I say this. Because all they hear is, "You can't pursue all those different ideas. You have to pick one." But that's not what I'm saying at all. You should never toss out your dreams. You should never have to pick one for the rest of your life. I mean, that's just crazy pants. What I've learned, though, is that you should pick one *for right now*. I know people think life is short, but I like to think life is long. I believe you will have ample time to do everything you want. There are so many examples of artists leveraging their success in one area to another area and expanding their creativity and income streams. Take Kristen Bell, for example. She started as an actress. Kristen worked on TV shows, and then made her way to starring in movies. After building an illustrious career as an actress, she expanded into building a production company. Now, Kristen and her husband Dax even have a line of baby products at Walmart. Kristen has also booked commercials and other product deals. She's built a pretty incredible career! But can you imagine if she did all of those things on a Tuesday? Like, some random Tuesday, when she was just starting out, she decided to audition for TV shows, build a production company, and get funding and launch a baby line for Walmart? All while, likely, also working a day job? I mean, I don't even know if Superwoman could do all that in a day.

Pursuing multiple interests at one time, especially while working a day job, is usually your subconscious' way of keeping you from succeeding at the thing you really want. It's a cop out in disguise. When your plate is that full, guess what usually gets put on the back burner? The one you're the most scared to do (and likely, the one you want the most). It's easy to push that real dream to the side and say, "I'll get to it later," and then focus on all the other "easier" things. Ohhh does your subconscious LOVE the "easier" things. The easier path. The dream-adjacent. And it will convince you that these easier things are totally worth it because in some wildly construed way, it will "lead to your dream."

Recently, I worked with a woman who had three different interests that she was pursuing at once: acting, writing and selling a screenplay, and building a business. She said that it was her personality to pursue multiple things at a time. And oh, by the way, she hasn't done anything with acting in awhile. It's been on the back burner. Even feeling like it's your personality to do multiple things at once is a fancy way to say, "My subconscious is distracting me from working on the one thing I really, really want." I'm not saying you can't pursue multiple things at once... if you literally have all the time in the world, don't need a day job, and are incredibly disciplined, then go for it! But most people don't have that kind of time and are not that disciplined. And remember what we said about being busy? It's often a distraction from what's really going on beneath the surface (like fear of failing).

While we're here, I have to talk about building an online business when you're an artist. I've spoken about this many times on video (you can go watch on my YouTube channel!) because I'm so passionate about this topic. Mostly because I want people to achieve their dreams and if I see people self-sabotaging, I have to swoop in and at least let them know.

If you're reading this book because you want to start a business and you're an entrepreneur, you can skip this paragraph. This is for the artists who want to act, sing, dance, write, direct, or create any other form of art for a living. In the past ten years, online businesses have become very popular. Anything from ecommerce, to courses, to coaching, has become very desirable because of the "get-rich-quick" schemes that advertise them. And I get it. Because, you know, I have one of those online businesses. But it's not something I'm doing on the side. It's my purpose. It's my mission. It's my main thing. And one thing you're not told about these businesses is that they take a lot of damn work. Just as much work as an acting career (or any other creative endeavor). Building a business has its perks, but I promise you, it's not a magic bullet. People see coaches shouting, "I made $10,000 this month!" and think it's easy and repeatable and a windfall of consistent money. But it. Takes. Work. And not even just tangible work like marketing, growing an email list, creating free content, etc. But also mental work. Selling an online product that is based off of *you* requires a ton of inner work, just like you need to do for your actual dream. Running a business is a full time job. And it will never be as mindless as a regular day job.

I have to tell you this because you may be tempted to start an online business as a way to make money on the side while you go for your dream. You want control. You're tired of waiting tables or driving for Postmates. I get it. But it's often a form of self-sabotage because the business could derail your dream for five years or more. One of my clients is living proof. She moved to Los Angeles to pursue her screenwriting dream, and five years later, she hasn't really done anything except write a bit and maybe take a class. She started an online business so she could support herself financially while she pursued this dream, but she didn't realize how much work the business took. No one is giving you a paycheck every week, you need to create it for yourself. So you're constantly working on creating that money every month. All of these years flew by, with no real progress on her dream.

Another guy I spoke to once, had a horrible thing happen as he tried to do something similar. He thought he would go into business with his friend to sell things on Amazon. They invested thousands of dollars and were sold these credit cards that ended up being fraudulent. They lost a bunch of money and a year of their time. Can you imagine if he spent that same amount of time and money on his dream, how much further along he'd be? And again, (this should become a drinking game...take a shot every time I say this) it all comes down to your belief in your success being inevitable. If you truly believed that you were going to succeed at your dream, without a doubt, you wouldn't spend thousands of dollars or years of your life pursuing anything else. You would see all of that as a distraction, and something that would delay the thing you want. Instead of investing $5,000 in a course or a program on how to start a business, why not invest that $5,000 into your dream?

A question I always ask my clients when they say they want to start a business is: What does your dream life look like? When you are successfully doing your art and getting paid for it, living your best life, what does that look like? Are you doing your art full time and also running this business? If the business is part of that dream life, then go for it! If you don't see it as part of that end-goal dream, then you may want to reevaluate your reasoning for wanting to start this business.

I've had many stumbles on my dream pursuit, but one thing that I know I'm really good at, is not even entertaining the idea that this won't work out. I don't have time for that. I don't want to waste time worrying about this not working. When I moved to LA and needed to find a day job, my parents suggested getting a Graphic Design job at a design firm. Since I had a degree in design, it seemed like a logical step to take. But I refused. I knew that having a 9-5 job that wasn't even in the TV industry was going to delay my dream. I had to be available during the day to cold email people, and I also needed to be able to give notice in as little as a day because TV turnaround happens very quickly. You're not always given two weeks or more until a job starts. If I spent time entertaining the thought that my TV dreams wouldn't happen, I would have gotten a design job. And chances are, I would work in that design job for years, maybe even get promoted, and never break into TV. I. Don't. Have. Time. For. That. I only have time for my dreams.

I want you to believe that there are endless doors for you to knock on. I want you to believe that it's inevitable that many of those doors will open. To quote Abraham again, "People get to the dock and they think they missed their boat. But there is always another one coming." Opportunities are available to you at this very moment. Which ones will you knock on?

*Eleven*

# THE TRUTH ABOUT REJECTION

In the summer between junior and senior year of high school, I went to UCLA for their summer theater intensive. And let me tell you, when our plane landed in sunny California, I could not have been more of a Los Angeles cliché. Even before we exited the plane, I felt this sparkly feeling run through me. I turned to my friend Steve, who was doing the program with me, and said, "OMG!! We're here! We're in LOS ANGELES!!!! Can you believe it??!" I didn't realize that not everyone shared my childlike enthusiasm until I heard his response: "Uh huh. Yeah." If I was at a 10 (and let's be honest I was way past 10), he was at a 1.

Seven years later, when I landed in Los Angeles for my permanent move, I felt just as tingly. Even though I was slightly terrified, I still had this feeling that I was entering a magical land once again. It wasn't even just that I believed every ounce of glamour that the media shoved down our throats about this city, but it was also the place where movies and TV shows were made. Like, *real* movies! The kind where they yell, "Action!" and "Cut!" It was so magical to me and I couldn't believe I was now so physically close to it.

So, of course, when I gathered my luggage and headed to the exit, I saw a TV show filming. The Universe was supporting my romanticized version of LA, and I couldn't be happier about it. As I walked through the airport doors, I saw director's chairs on the sidewalk. It was my first opportunity to act breezy in front of celebrities—you know, where I pretend to not care and be cool, but secretly straining my eyes so hard to make out the name of the show and the actors on set. Breezy like Monica Geller. As I got closer, I saw that it was *Entourage*. Even though I didn't really watch the show, I knew it was hugely popular, so it was the perfect show to brag about back home. You know, first day—first *hour*, even—in Los Angeles, and I walk right past the *Entourage* set. No big deal!

Fast forward a few months, and my bosses asked me to design some graphics for *Entourage*. The show I was working on (my very first show ever!) was run by the *Entourage* crew. While *Entourage* was on hiatus between seasons, the crew came over to our show. The Universe never stops sending those winks! It all felt too crazy to be coincidental.

While I only worked on a couple of episodes of *Entourage*, I felt like part of the family. I got to hang out at E's house. I got to eat steak from the fancy catering (because by season eight they could afford the good stuff). And most of the crew became my friends. It was so crazy that months prior, I was walking off the plane to start this new life, watching this show film. It felt magical. Like my dreams were coming true in the fairytale way I believed in. But, of course, all fairytales come to an end. Several months later, my dreamy bubble popped and I was devastated.

When my show ended for the season (and was later cancelled), the *Entourage* crew went back to *Entourage*. I thought, for sure, I could work with them. There was an opening in the art department for an assistant, and I was so excited to interview. I mean, I was a shoe in, right?! I was at E's house! I ate the steak! I had the friends! And I had even designed graphics for them before. There was no way this job wasn't mine.

But it wasn't. Shortly after the interview, I found out I didn't get the job. Some other girl named Jackie got the job. She knew a producer or something—her connections were higher up than mine. I didn't know the details, all I knew was this was my first Hollywood rejection and it sucked. I questioned my talent. I questioned my personality. Was I not good enough? How did this happen? Even with all my connections, they still didn't want me. I was devastated and took it personally.

Many years later, when I was in the union, cruising along on lots of TV shows, a friend reached out to me. She said, "Hey Erica! I have this friend, Jackie, who is looking for some advice on getting into the union. Could you talk to her?" Yes, *that* Jackie. I could feel the old insecurities come brimming to the surface. But years had passed, and I'm a nice person. So, of course I said "Yes." And I revelled in the irony: this girl who beat me out for a job was now needing my help to advance her career. Good thing I had practice being the "bigger person."

## TRUTH #1

When Jackie and I connected, I melted into a puddle of shame. She was the sweetest girl who was so much like me. Jackie was an artist who loved design. She also loved to sing and wrote her own music (I did this too, during my depression years...more on that later). One year, we even wore the same Halloween costume! Our similarities were endless and helped me let my guard down and welcome Jackie in. I'm so glad I did, because she told me something that changed the way I viewed rejection forever...

As Jackie and I became friends, we talked about that fateful *Entourage* job. It turns out that Jackie met her husband on that show. *She met her husband!* I mean, holy crap! Talk about there being a reason Jackie had to get that job over me. Since then, Jackie has had two kids with her husband. I went to one of her baby showers. It blows my mind to think that if I got that job, those babies may not exist! Jackie's love story may not exist! And I finally understood that the rejection had absolutely nothing to do with me. It was Jackie's time. My time would come later. **This is Truth #1: Rejection is rarely personal.**

There are so many factors that go into a decision and you not being good enough or likeable enough is rarely one of those factors. It's hardly ever about you, and more about what they were looking for, or someone else having a connection, or even hiring a "name" (known artist or celebrity). And remember, you were meant for this, so eventually it *has* to work out. If it's not this time, that's okay. There are so many more opportunities available to you.

That doesn't mean it doesn't hurt. I know the pain of rejection. Trust me, I know it well. From my design professor not believing in me, to my high school theater teacher agreeing I wasn't good enough, to not being asked back on a show, to all of the other rejections I received throughout my career...I. KNOW. I've cried ugly tears. The kind with mascara running down my face. I've asked the Universe why I was being punished. I've felt unworthy. I've felt unlovable. And if I'm being really honest, some of those feelings came up as recently as last week. Even though I'm an expert in this stuff, I'm also a human being who messes up. I think it's important for you to know that, because I don't want you to feel like you're incapable of big success if you have a few days where you're crying rejection tears. It's really easy for me to write words that say "rejection is protection" and move on. But I know that it's messier than that. I know we're not robots, and no matter how much inner work we do, we still might need a good cry one day.

I do think that having the tools to move through your life like a High Achiever will help immensely. I always teach my clients that it's okay to feel your feelings—whatever comes up. Our goal isn't to never feel rejected again. Our goal is to shorten the time those feelings envelop us and stop us from moving forward. That last time I felt rejected and cried? I turned it around in merely minutes. The more I do that and use these tools, the shorter the time I feel discouraged. I mean, *minutes*! We're talking minutes here! It used to take me *months*. So to be down to minutes, is not only a great accomplishment, but more importantly, gets me in the energy of action and success much faster. This can lead to opportunities, money, and relationships that I would have otherwise missed out on. I know actors who were dropped by their agent and felt sorry for themselves for an entire year. I know artists who didn't book a job and let the discouragement turn into depression that lasted more than 6 months. Every time we do this—let the rejection take over—we are literally missing out on new opportunities and leaving money on the table.

## TRUTH #2
Back in high school, I had a huge crush on this guy in the drama club.

(Yes, I was a full-on theater nerd!) As you can probably tell, I tend to wear my heart on my sleeve, so I don't think it was a secret amongst our friends that I had these crushy feelings. Whenever I saw him, my heart would do that glowy thing that they do on *Jane The Virgin*. And oh my gosh, even seeing his screen name pop up on AOL Instant Messenger made me feel butterflies (yes, I'm old). This couldn't be more of a cliché high school crush. One night, I attended a theater cast party with my friends and it was a big sleepover. (My high school experience was very PG, so don't be afraid of what comes next. LOL). We were all in a big room together, and I got to sleep next to my crush!! I mean, hello dreams. I was so excited just to be near him. Then, it happened. Before we fell asleep, he pulled me closer to him and kissed me! O-M-G! I had hearts in my eyes and I was so happy. That's all that happened, because, like I said, very PG, but in my mind, I was practically planning our wedding. Ok, maybe not that far, but I definitely told my girlfriends and assumed he and I would now be boyfriend and girlfriend. But there was a plot twist I didn't see coming. The next school day, I found out that this guy told all of our friends that the kiss never happened. He denied it. He pretended like this moment I had been dreaming of never even happened. It was one of the first times I felt completely rejected and unworthy. It was like he was ashamed of me. And this feeling would come up again and again over the course of my life.

In my current adult life, I noticed (with the help of therapy) that any time something small happened that felt like a personal rejection, I would immediately recall those feelings from high school and feel that rejection all over again. This is what Dr. Joe Dispenza explains as memorized reactions. An impactful moment happens once, creating a deep memory, and then that memory is fired as a chemical reaction throughout our body every time we have a similar experience. It becomes unconscious—we aren't consciously choosing these thoughts and feelings, they are habitually happening without our control. Think about when you're driving—when you drive a car, you're not thinking about whether the brake or the gas is on the left. Your foot just knows which one to press because you've been doing it for so long. So you can do other things while driving...listen to the radio, check your blind spot, or have a conversation. Your conscious mind doesn't have to think about your feet, that's happening unconsciously. It's the same thing with your memorized reactions. In my case, my conscious mind doesn't have to think about the rejection because my unconscious mind has already sent the signals to tell my brain and body what to do. This means that every time I experience a personal rejection, I'm not in the driver's seat (pun intended). I don't have control over how I react. My reaction is memorized. It's recalled and refired.

It wasn't until a therapy session, where I realized this reaction was being fired even when it wasn't warranted. I would feel rejected at a tiny hint of dismissal (like an email or a text not getting a response) and the reaction would begin. It didn't even give me time to realize that many of these instances weren't actually rejection. My mind created stories to make it fit the narrative I was used to. I would be taken back to that moment in high school all over again. I would literally lose sleep over these experiences, thinking I was rejected again and feeling unworthy and unlovable. This is how the second truth was solidified for me. **Truth #2: Rejection isn't painful. It's the stories we tell ourselves about what the rejection means, that is painful.**

As you move through your dream pursuit, you will experience rejection. It's inevitable, as long as you're putting yourself out there. This is a good thing because if you're putting yourself in a position to get rejected, that means you're also putting yourself in a position to get a "yes." Every time you get the rejection letter, or email, or response, it's easy to go down a rabbit hole of what that rejection means. We tend to create an entire story (I mean, we are creative artists, after all!) that says, "I'm not good enough. This will never happen for me. They didn't like me. I'm not likable. I'm not worthy of their time. I'm not worthy of success. Something must be wrong with me." We fill in the blanks and decide that we know what this rejection means. But it's fiction. None of it is based in truth or data. We're creating a narrative that doesn't actually exist. And it may even be triggered by past rejections from our childhood, making our new fictional story a memorized habit.

Instead of feeling sorry for yourself when you're rejected, take a step back and stop writing that story you're crafting. Any rejection says absolutely nothing about your potential. Your ability to achieve your dreams is not determined by any one rejection. It's determined by *you*, and you alone.

## TRUTH #3

If we take a look at any successful person in history, their paths are littered with rejections. Lisa Kudrow was fired from *Frasier*. Fired! She booked a role on a pilot expected to be a hit and was freaking fired. Guess what she booked after that? *Friends*. Melissa McCarthy put on a comedy show with her friends early in her career and only one person showed up to sit in the audience. One! Melissa McCarthy is now one of the highest paid actresses in Hollywood. J.K. Rowling's original *Harry Potter* pitch was rejected 12 times. Harry Freaking Potter! The people who rejected that one must be kicking themselves. Bill Gates' first software company failed. Like, lost money. Then he founded Microsoft. Meryl Streep was rejected for a role in the movie *King Kong*. The producer said she was too ugly. Now Meryl Streep has been nominated for 21 Oscars. Twenty-freaking-one! I can also tell you that of the 38 television shows and films I've worked on, I never once booked the job from an interview (I don't count that very first show because even though they interviewed me, they didn't interview anyone else. It was more of a formality.). I've had four TV interviews throughout my career and I never got the job from any of them. Are you seeing a pattern here? **This is Truth #3: Rejection is literally what success stories are made of.**

Every time you experience rejection, you can pat yourself on the back and trust that this is part of the process. You're on your way! As Jack Canfield says, "SW, SW, SW, SW: Some will, some won't. So what? Someone's waiting." With every "No" you get, you're one step closer to your "Yes." And one day, you'll be accepting your award, or giving a graduation commencement, and you'll tell the stories of all the times you were rejected, and how it led you to where you are today because you kept going and you never stopped believing in yourself...

## TRUTH #4

...Which brings me to the final truth about rejection. **Truth #4: Rejection usually leads to something better.** Instead of "Rejection is protection" and thinking that a rejection is protecting you from something bad, I like to think that it's leading you to something better. It's the glass-half-full version. The Universe knows your deepest desires and it's always leading you to them. The Universe knows what's in your highest good and will deliver that to you every time (as long as you're working with it, which is a story for another chapter). One of Abraham Hicks' famous mantras is, "Everything is always working out for me." When I get a rejection, I ask, "What if this is for a reason? What if this is leading to something else?" I believe it's going to work out and that I'll be led to something even more exciting. Like that time I wasn't asked back to a show, and then was hired on *Chasing Life* and felt ten times happier. The Universe was like, *Erica, I have to get you out of here*

*because it's not in alignment with your dreams. I've got something else for*
*you that you'll love, just follow me.*

Rejection is only upsetting when it triggers our fears and insecurities. To combat that, all you have to do is have an unwavering belief in yourself and your success. I know that may be easier said than done, but practice it. It's like a muscle that you build. Work it, baby. Here are some steps you can take as you work on your belief:

1.  Allow yourself to feel your feelings, without judgement. Whatever comes up, comes up. No shame necessary.

2.  Stop the negative story spiral in its track with affirmations: My success is inevitable. I am talented. I am amazing. My dream opportunity is just around the corner. There is an abundance of opportunities available to me.

3.  Go do something fun that is completely unrelated to your dream. What lights you up? What makes you laugh? Get out of the rejected energy you feel by stepping into a new energy. Have a game night with your friends. Play with your dog. Take yourself out on a date. It's easier to go "general" and feel good about something unrelated than to force good feelings about the rejection. Make your energy your priority. Always. Every action you take should be from an excited, confident energy.

4.  Let yourself be led to your next inspired action (and that inspiration will only come once you've done Step 3). Don't skip Step 3 because taking action from an uninspired, desperate place will not produce the dreamy results you want. Let yourself be inspired into action so it comes from a place of love, rather than fear.

Rejection should be celebrated. It's proof that you're putting yourself out there and taking risks. It puts you one step closer to getting that "Yes." You can cry that ugly cry and feel sorry for yourself for a moment, but then remember the truth about rejection: It's rarely personal. It's not painful, it's the stories you tell yourself about what the rejection means that is painful. It's literally what success stories are made of, and it's often leading you to something better. Now *that* is something to smile about! Pop the cork, let's have some champagne, you were rejected! Here comes the big success.

# Twelve

# THE SECRET WEAPON TO GETTING WHAT YOU WANT

Asking for what you want seems way too bold for most people (especially women). So instead, we ask for a tiny piece of what we want. Or something close-ish to what we want. I mean, we don't want to step on any toes! How dare we ask for the exact thing that we desire!

I know that big dreams feel unattainable. They feel so far away and out of reach, that you may as well take whatever you can get. The thing you actually want is too hard, too impossible. So you reach for something easier. The problem is, that easier thing never feels good. It feels like a scrap because it *is* a scrap. Those crumbs you're thrown feel crummy (see what I did there? Gosh, I'm so clever) and it's okay to admit that. You don't have to pretend to feel elated at the fact that you got something that is a miniscule fraction of what you actually want.

It's time to change all of that. You hear me? It's time to start asking for what you want. It's time to start believing you're worthy of what you want. It's time to start believing it's possible to get what you want. Enter, my secret weapon: The Clear Intentions List.

## THE CLEAR INTENTIONS LIST

While I'm calling this list the Secret Weapon, you may also call it common sense. It shouldn't be mind blowing, but it is because most people aren't doing it. The Clear Intentions List is exactly what it sounds like: a list of the intentions you'd like to set for whatever opportunity comes your way. Whether it's an interview for a job, a meeting with an investor, a coffee with a new connection, or your next gig. Whatever you have coming up, it's time to decide what you want from it.

The birth of this list came from watching my clients go through less-than-ideal relationships with agents. They would say, "I have an agent and they are really nice! But they hardly ever answer my emails." Or, "I have an offer from an agent! We don't really click and they don't seem to be on board with my big vision, but they are the only offer I have, so I'll take it!" They were settling for agents that weren't what they actually wanted. And they settled because they didn't believe that what they wanted was possible. They thought it was too much to ask for an agent who was great and communicated. It was a slew of "But relationships," as my friend Jason calls it. He says there are two kinds of relationships: the And relationship, and the But relationship. The But relationship is: *My partner is so funny and smart! But they don't make time for me.* The And relationship is: *My partner is so funny and smart! And they treat me so well! And they support my dreams!* It doesn't mean there aren't any issues that arise with the And relationship, but overall it's all good. The But relationship is what so many of us fall into—not just in relationships, but in opportunities, jobs, etc. We're only partly satisfied but we believe that's all we can get or all we deserve, so we accept it.

The Clear Intentions List is your chance to start clean. It's your chance to ask for what you want...*exactly* what you want. It's also your chance to map out best-case scenarios. When a client of mine had a big meeting coming up with a well-known movie producer, he made a Clear Intentions List for all the scenarios he dreamed would come from this meeting. It was everything from "I get to go into development with this producer" to "He connects me to another producer who could help me get these scripts off the ground." It was a range from "This would be the absolute BEST thing to come out of this meeting!" to "This smaller thing would still be great because it would give me forward momentum." My client ended up getting his best-case scenario and has been working with this producer developing projects for the past two years.

In the next chapter, you'll begin connecting with people, so now is the time to set your intentions for what you'd like to come out of these connections. A small disclaimer: this isn't a list of you forcing how this must come about. You don't want to be so white-knuckled around how your dream unfolds, you want to leave room for the magic. When you have a meeting or opportunity, it may turn out better than anything you wrote down on your list...something you couldn't even dream up. And you want to make space for that possibility. This list is a chance for you to start asking for what you want—from the Universe, and from the person with whom you're connecting. You want to start intentionally guiding your dream pursuit so it isn't a mishmosh of "whatever I can get"s. Be calculated. Be strategic.

It's also great to do this for people. Like I mentioned before with agents, you can also do this for coworkers or collaborators. Set your intention for what you want that experience or relationship to feel like.

(And while we're at it, you can do this for dating, too, if you haven't already figured that out!) To get started with your Clear Intentions List, ask yourself the question, "Wouldn't it be cool if...?" and write down whatever comes to you. Like, "Wouldn't it be cool if this meeting led to my next steps?" Or "I really wish...". Like, "I really wish I had an agent who fully supported my overall vision and was great with communication." This is how you can begin making your Clear Intentions List.

Mike Dooley, author of *Playing the Matrix*, says that a great way to manifest what you desire is to let go of the specific title and, instead, embrace the feelings you want to feel. I think this is especially important when you're writing your Clear Intentions List because it's easy to get attached to a specific outcome. For example, an actor might say they want to be repped by CAA (one of the top agencies in the industry). Instead of setting that specific intention, I would tell the actor to make a list of all the reasons why they want to be repped by CAA. Their list might look something like this:

### CAA (Creative Arts Agency)
- Has great connections with casting directors and other filmmakers
- Reps other successful actors
- Their reputation helps get their actors opportunities
- Because they rep many types of creatives, they could introduce me to writers or directors that I could collaborate with

Makes sense why they would want CAA, right? After the actor makes this list, it's time to delete "CAA" from the top. The list stays the same, but the "CAA" title goes away. When you remove that agency title, you're left with your intentions that are no longer attached to a specific outcome. We often don't realize that we would be totally fulfilled if we got all of the qualities we were looking for but it came in a different package. With this agency example, the actor could be repped by Paradigm and that still fulfills all the qualities they are looking for. By removing "CAA," they are opening themselves up to endless possibilities **that will still give them everything they want.** What you really want is everything on your list—not the label you give it. When we attach ourselves to a specific outcome, we are shutting ourselves off from all the other doors around us and insisting we only knock on one. This makes your goals narrow-minded and more difficult to achieve.

So make your Clear Intentions List but let go of the specific titles. Write down everything you're looking for—like your "Must love dogs" list. Set the intentions. Ask for what you want. And don't say "Yes" to anything that doesn't match this list. This doesn't mean that you should turn down opportunities that aren't the really big ones you want...I recognize there is a bridge to cross, and sometimes there are milestones to hit before the really big one. It just means you should stop settling for things that feel shitty, and start trusting that you are allowed to receive things that feel good and exciting. One of my clients recently got two representation offers and had to choose one. She felt pulled towards one of the managers and entered negotiations over the contract. My client was very insistent on asking for what she wanted, so it took some time to go back and forth, but the manager was patient and accommodating and made it work. My client signed the contract a few weeks later. I know it can feel really scary to turn down something just because it doesn't feel aligned with all your desires. But it only feels scary when you believe there are no more offers coming. When you feel a prisoner to this one and only opportunity because you don't believe others will come along, that's when the desperation kicks in and you accept any crumbs thrown your way. Remember, we live in an abundant world. There will always be more opportunities because...oh, hey...you create your reality. That means you created this opportunity, so you can create others. This opportunity was not some lucky thing that you had no involvement in. You created it. You can create it again.

## THE HUMBLE BRAG

Making your Clear Intentions List is a great way to ask for what you want in your mind, or on a piece of paper. But how do you do it when you're actually in front of another human being? The other day on a webinar I was teaching, one of the attendees asked, "I've made some high level connections from my last project, and I'm getting meetings with them. But every time I get in front of them, I tend to freeze up. How can I stop doing this?" I thought this was a great question because so many people can relate. When you get an opportunity, how can you play it cool? The thing is, we tend to freeze up because we feel inadequate. The opportunity feels bigger or higher than us and we feel our insecurities triggered. We might feel afraid to talk because we don't want to say the wrong thing, or maybe we suddenly have no idea what to say. The self doubt takes over. When we're in that self doubt, the desperation kicks in. We feel ourselves in the, "Please pick me!" energy. We look for validation, "Please tell me I'm worthy of your time! Tell me I'm good enough!" You probably already know this, but that's not the sexiest energy. Confidence is much more attractive.

Building your confidence in yourself is the first thing you should do before one of those meetings. I asked the attendee, "Do you freeze up when you're talking to your friends?" He responded, "No, of course not." So I continued, "What makes this different? It's just a conversation." The difference is the power dynamic. It felt like this new contact had power over him. This contact was more experienced and more well-known. So the attendee felt inadequate, causing him to freeze up. When you feel inadequate or insecure, it's pretty hard to stick to your

Clear Intentions List. Know what I mean? How do you confidently ask for what you want when you can barely utter any normal words?

This is a great time to connect to your Star Power. Remember all that work you did in the first half of this book? Time to do it again! As you prepare to put your Clear Intentions List into play, it's time to feel worthy of everything you want. Even if you have less experience than whomever you're comparing yourself to, it doesn't mean that what you're selling doesn't have incredible value. Whether you're pitching your ideas, selling your art, connecting with potential collaborators, or making an offer to a customer, you have to believe in what you're selling. Let me give you two scenarios to sell this book...tell me which one you would buy:

1. Hey! I wrote this book that is good for anyone with a dream. I think maybe you'll like it. I mean, my Mom liked it. I put a lot of work into it. It's not as good as some of the other self help books out there, or I mean, maybe it is, but I still think you'll like it. It's my first time writing so if it sucks, that's why. But I'm working on it! - OR -

2. Hey! I am SO EXCITED to share *Meant For This* with you! This book will change your life. I'm so proud of the system I created and how it has helped hundreds of artists achieve their dreams. The system even works in Hollywood, one of the hardest industries to succeed in! My clients have booked TV shows and films on every major network (like Netflix, Hulu, HBO, etc.) by using the exact system in this book! I mean, can you imagine how you'll feel when you're living your dream? It doesn't matter how big your dream is, or how "impossible" people think it is, I'm telling you, this book will make it happen. Your life will be split into two segments:

Before reading *Meant For This*, and After reading *Meant For This*. And those two segments will look vastly different.

...So which scenario sells the book better? Which one makes you want to buy? As you can see, the first scenario is from a person who is lacking confidence in what they're selling. They are nervous and looking for validation. They also use a defense mechanism to protect themselves in case the book is perceived as bad.

The second scenario comes from someone who really believes in what they're selling. Oh, hey, that's me! Can you see the difference? When you head into your meetings or connect with potential "customers" (whatever your dream is), you want to have confidence and believe in what you're selling. By the way, what you're selling could be yourself. If you're submitting yourself to get an agent or manager, you're selling yourself. You are the product. And you need to believe that your product is badass and worthy of the thing you're seeking.

When you don't feel worthy, it will be reflected back to you. Go back to that first scenario about my book. What do you think a person's response would be to buying my book? They might be like, "Eh, no thanks..." and that would feel like confirmation that I'm not good enough or my book isn't good enough. It's the energy I put out, so it would be the energy I get back.

Instead of living in the "Please choose me!" energy, you want to first choose yourself. No one else needs to validate you. When you believe in yourself and what you have to offer, you are the only one who needs to validate you. You don't need someone to choose you because you choose yourself. It is the opposite of desperate. It's trusting that if this opportunity isn't a match, that's totally okay! It's not because you're not worthy. It just wasn't the right fit. But there are so many more opportunities around the corner. Plus, the more you choose yourself and feel confident in what you're selling, the more *that* will be reflected back to you and you'll get that "yes" much faster.

Enter: the Humble Brag. Once you feel good about yourself, your product, your value, etc., it's time to communicate that to your customer (I keep using this word but it doesn't have to translate into a literal customer...translate it to your dream). In order to get what you want from your Clear Intentions List, you have to communicate why you're worth all of those things. This can be tricky because most of us have been taught all our lives not to brag. We're taught to be humble and not show off. Bragging can seem arrogant and is unnecessary. While that makes sense in social situations, it can limit your ability to talk about your accomplishments and value in a way that will get your customer on board. Selling is not the time to hold back (as illustrated with my book scenarios).

It's time to start bragging! But, in a less obnoxious way, of course. You don't need to be like, "Look how amazing I am!!!!!!" but you do need to say, "Here's why I am so great!" Do you see the difference? You're not bragging for bragging's sake. You're communicating the reasons you bring value to the table. Just like with the second book scenario, I told you that:

- My book will change your life
- It contains a proven system that works in Hollywood
- My clients have booked jobs on every major network
- It has helped hundreds of artists achieve their dreams
- It doesn't matter how "impossible" your dream is, this book will help you

This isn't arrogantly bragging—this is a list of reasons why my book is worth buying. So why are you worth buying (or working with)? Why is your art valuable? Also notice that I listed things a reader might be looking for: a reader may want to work in Hollywood; they may be an artist who wants to achieve their dreams; they may have been told their dream is "impossible." I'm hitting pain points and desires of my ideal reader. So these are calculated brags.

When you think about your value, what do you bring to the table that your audience may be looking for? For example, when an actor submits to an agent, an agent may be looking for someone who already has some experience. They may be looking for proof that they book work and perform well. So an actor could say, "I've already booked over 10 short films in the past few years, and two of them have gone on to win awards at major festivals." See how that solves the problem of what the agent might be looking for?

Whenever you have an opportunity...a meeting, an interview, a coffee with a connection, submitting yourself for a job, you want to brag about yourself in a way that hits what the other party is looking for. Let them know why you are the perfect person for this opportunity. Let go of the childhood rule that bragging is bad. Now is your time to shine. Build your confidence. Talk about yourself or your project like it's the best thing since sliced bread. Confidence is contagious and the more you believe in what you're selling, the more your customer will believe in what you're selling. And once you share how awesome you are, it becomes much easier to whip out that Clear Intentions List and ask for what you want.

## EDUCATE PEOPLE ON HOW YOU WANT TO BE SEEN

Here's another thing: you have to educate people on how you want to be seen. Don't wait for others to decide how you're seen. You need to control that narrative. Just like the tabloids used to control the celebrity narrative, but now celebrities have taken back their power by sharing their own truths on social media. When I was starting out in this industry, I decided not to pursue a middle-level job of Art Coordinator because I noticed that every TV show I worked on, the Art Coordinator was always seen as an Art Coordinator, even if that wasn't their end-goal position. People on the crew saw the Coordinator as the Coordinator and never saw them as anything else. So if you were a Coordinator and you really wanted to be a Graphic Designer, you needed to tell everyone, "I'm a designer." If you didn't, the assumption was made for you. I didn't want to risk that, so I educated everyone around me and told them I was a designer. This can also work with experience level—not that you should lie about your experience, but if you come across as confident and tell people the title you want, they're more likely to see you there, regardless if you have experience in that position.

## STOP "ASPIRING"

And while we're on this, please drop the word "aspiring" from your title. I know the common narrative says that you need paying jobs in order to drop that word, but I think that's complete bullshit. I also think that ties your identity to "aspiring," therefore holding you back energetically and mentally. If you are an artist...meaning, you make art...then you are an artist. You are not aspiring just because you haven't been paid yet (or at a certain level). Own what you want. This comes back to educating people on how you want to be seen. If you met someone in a meeting and said, "I'm an aspiring writer" it gives off a very different vibe than, "I'm a writer." You are the only one who can validate yourself. You decide who you are and what you're worth.

Write your Clear Intentions List. Decide what you want. Access your Star Power and feel worthy of those things. And then tell people why you're worthy of them. You are so much more incredible than you're allowing yourself to feel. Start choosing yourself. It's about damn time!

# Thirteen

# HOW TO MAKE
# ~~CONNECTIONS~~
# RELATIONSHIPS

A million years ago (okay, maybe twelve), I was sitting at home in my parent's house in a suburban town outside of Philly. I was watching a classic—*13 Going On 30*—and I jumped up with excitement over an aha moment. (Later, I discovered that part of the information in this aha moment was not true, but just let me tell my story because it still works.) So I was watching the scene where Jenna and Matt (Jennifer Garner and Mark Ruffalo) are walking through the streets sharing a box of their favorite candy, Razzles. And that's when it hit me. "OMG!! A graphic designer had to have designed that fake candy box! OMG I can design graphics for movies!" It was a light bulb moment, to say the least. I was bursting with excitement over this discovery.

If you're good at spotting false information, then you probably already know that Razzles are, in fact, a real candy. But you're smarter than me. I didn't know this, I thought it was a fictional candy, and if it was fictional, a graphic designer had to have designed the box. Even though I was wrong about the candy, I wasn't wrong about how graphics work in movies and television. There are many instances in which that *would* be a fictional candy and a graphic designer would design the box. In fact, small tidbit for you, it's more likely to happen in television because traditional television has commercials, so a show can't have any products that may compete with the products in the advertisements during commercial breaks. Unless it's product placement and a show has permission, the products need to be fictional names. That's what keeps a designer so busy in television! Anyway, this was my big moment of realizing my true dream. I now knew what I wanted to do with my design degree once I graduated college.

There was only one teeny, tiny problem. I lived 3,000 miles away from Los Angeles and didn't know a soul in the industry. Since I heard that Hollywood was so dependent on connections, I was basically screwed. Or, as I saw it, presented with a pretty big obstacle. How on earth was I going to break into an industry without any connections? Then my second big aha moment came: I could make my own connections through the power of the internet.

So I started out on a massive search: I scoured IMDb for graphic designers on all the TV shows I loved or knew of. I sat through the long movie credits in the theater. Once I compiled a list of names, I set out to find their email addresses or their social media profiles. The internet put all this information at my fingertips, so I felt excited with the possibilities. One by one, I began cold emailing them. "How are graphic designers hired? Is it a design firm or a person who does this?" I asked them. I had no idea how the industry worked and I thought those answers would help give me my next steps. Some people were really nice and answered my questions. Many people didn't respond. And then one day I messaged a guy on Facebook...

- *Hey! Did you work on Entourage?* (Funny how Entourage keeps coming up, right?!) *I saw your name on IMDb and wasn't sure if you were him.*
- Yes, that's me!
- *I think I'll be in LA the week of July 8th. Would it be possible to meet with you and show you my portfolio?*
- Portfolio's great!! You'll definitely fit in out here, just be prepared to work fast and crazy.

And my first connection in LA was born. This connection helped me get my first TV show. Over time, this connection became a friend. Then that friend helped me book more TV shows over the course of eight years. That friend turned into a mentor. And that's when I learned the power of relationships over connections.

The journey of a big dream is a long game. As much as we want everything to happen right this second, it's really a marathon, not a sprint. Connections may help you along the way, but raving fans who want to support you will go so much further. The thing to remember is that all people are humans. They have interests and personalities. Instead of looking for connections, look for **friends**. Tweak that title in your mind. A connection has the potential to become a genuine friend, and that genuine friend will love and support you and want to help you win.

Whatever you're pursuing, relationships will always be one of the keys to your success. Whether it's someone who hires you, someone who gets you in the door, or someone who connects you to an opportunity...you can't get far without people. Even if it's as simple as someone showing you your next steps, relationships are invaluable. I believe the Universe is always guiding us to these connections, but it also takes tangible work, like reaching out and making the ask. I've learned that the best way to build relationships is by meeting in person because it speeds up the trust and connection. But meeting in person isn't always possible, especially when you're starting out and don't know anyone. That's why the second best way is **cold emailing**.

I know, I know, it's scary. It's weird. You feel awkward, you don't know what to say. What if they hate you or find you annoying? First of all, I've got you on all of those. Second of all, you can certainly choose to use those fears as an excuse not to make connections. But we've already decided you're a High Achiever. You've got Star Power. So you're not gonna let a few fears of cold emailing stop you from living your best life and achieving your dreams. Am I right?! And remember that gratitude we felt for the internet because our parents or grandparents had to literally knock on doors in person? Yeah, I'll take cold emailing any day! Plus, I was able to do it from Philadelphia...3,000 miles away from the industry I wanted to be in. So you can do this anywhere. Any time.

When you're just starting out, you may not know who to contact, what to say, or what actions to take. If you have a lot of holes in your reverse engineer ladder, you might need help filling them. Like I said, when I started my dream pursuit, I had no idea how Hollywood worked. I didn't know how designers were hired. I didn't know what a union was. I didn't know the language. I had no idea what my first step should even be. So I started asking. I emailed people who were doing what I wanted to do, and I asked them. I call this the Rule of 10.

## THE RULE OF 10

The Rule of 10 says that if you don't know how to begin your journey (or what the next steps are), ask at least ten people for the answers. What I've found is that since there is no one-way to achieve a big dream, everyone breaks in differently. So if you ask ten people, you may get ten different answers. Or maybe you'll get 5 different answers repeated. Regardless of how many patterns you see, you should have enough information to make a calculated next step. If you get ten different answers, try all ten. Not necessarily at the same time, but use all ten as potential strategies. Remember, the more doors to knock on, the better.

That's why I cold emailed graphic designers. They were people who had the jobs I wanted, so they obviously knew what my first step need-ed to be. This was a great place to start, and I didn't even feel a ton of fear around making "connections" because I was just asking people questions. I wasn't asking for a job or for a meeting or anything big. I asked simple questions that were easy to answer. And the information I received helped inform my next moves.

So start by researching people. I would look for 1) people who are literally doing what you want to do; and 2) people who are connected to what you want to do (they could hire you or work with people like you). For example, let's say I was a fine artist and I wanted to get my paintings in a gallery but had no idea how to make that happen. I might email other artists who have had their work in galleries, and I might also email someone who works in a gallery.

Some of your questions may be Google-able, so I would start there. (People may get annoyed if you ask them something that can easily be found in a Google search.) But even if I found the answer via Google, I would still send a cold message to someone asking them to confirm my findings. Because the goal here is to get your next steps, and also begin to form relationships with people who can help you. Ideally, you find people with whom you naturally connect. Those people can become friends along the way. Remember, this is a long game.

Here are the steps to follow in this process:
1. Find people who are already doing what you want to do or who work closely with people like you.
2. Find their email address or their social media profiles.
3. Search the internet for your questions.
4. Cold message the people and ask them your questions or ask them to confirm your findings.

## STEP 1: FIND THE PEOPLE

There are many ways to find people to connect with, using the power of the internet. For Hollywood, I always start with IMDb. A good old fashioned Google search can do the trick, too. Look in trade magazines. News announcements. Even hashtags related to your industry on Instagram and Twitter. Competitions and festivals are a great place to look. Books you love, art you admire, speakers at events you attend. Potential connections are everywhere when you believe they are. It's easy to fall into the woe-is-me energy and complain that you don't have any connections. But when you're in that space, you'll never see the ones that are literally right in front of you.

One time, I attended a marketing seminar where the co-founder of Priceline.com gave a speech. After he finished talking, he put up a slide with his email address. I couldn't believe it! There were hundreds of people in the audience, so this was very generous. Immediately, I opened my phone and sent him an email. I let him know how much I enjoyed his speech and complemented one of the concepts he shared that impacted me. I received a nice response back and he suggested I keep in touch. I continued to follow up, and the next time he was in Los Angeles (an album he produced was nominated for a Grammy!), he took time to get coffee with me and I was able to ask him questions. He told me I was the only one he made time for during this trip because I was the only one who kept in touch and followed up. What an incredible opportunity that so many people missed out on! The connection was right there, up for grabs. But if you don't believe you're worthy of the meeting, or that you can do this, you'll never even see it.

Keep your eyes open. There are people all around you, available to you at this very moment, who want to help you with your dreams.

## STEP 2: FIND THEIR CONTACT INFORMATION

I feel like I don't even have to tell you all of this because Google has most of the answers, but I hope that by providing these examples, it will help you take action faster. I've been cold emailing people for over a decade, and I'll never stop! I think it's one of the most underrated tools in getting ahead. People avoid it because they're scared or because they don't have the patience to do it until they get a response. But it's the easiest, fastest way to break into your dream or your next level.

There are a lot of tools out there to help you find contact information. Obviously, there is social media. You can look them up on Facebook, Instagram, Twitter, and LinkedIn. They might even have their own website with contact information. For Hollywood contacts like agents, managers, publicists, and production companies, I use IMDb Pro. It's the paid version of IMDb and worth every penny.

There is also a tool called Rocket Reach. They have a free version that is a great way to find email addresses for people, especially if they work for a company. Even if you can't find a specific person on there, if you can find other people at the same company, you can see the formula for email addresses there (like firstname@company.com). You can use that formula to test their email address. (You can find all of these resources on my website at hollywoodsuccesscoach.com/mft-resources)

Many industries also have directories. For example, in Hollywood, the DGA (Director's Guild) has a public directory where you can look up any director, first AD, etc. Sometimes you'll find producers on there, too. Every single person may not be listed, but my clients have used this to get production jobs and it's worked really well. Look for directories in your industry. If you're in a union, your union might have a members-only directory that you can take advantage of.

Once you begin collecting contact information, start a spreadsheet. It's good to keep track when you start emailing dozens (or hundreds) of people.

## STEP 3: GOOGLE YOUR QUESTIONS

Just do it. Search the internet for answers before you ask someone. If you can't find the answers to your questions, that's a great time to send a cold email. If you do find the answers, take that information and send an email asking if it's correct.

## STEP 4: SEND THOSE COLD EMAILS!

Let's talk about what to say in your cold emails. This could vary depending on the goal of your email, but what I'm sharing here is mostly for connecting to new people and building relationships. My clients also use cold email for getting jobs, pitching their projects, and submitting to agents, but that's a whole different beast.

When you're focused on meeting new people, always follow the three B's: Be brief, Be complimentary, and Be specific. **Be Brief:** You should always assume that the person you're contacting is very busy, so you want to take up as little of their time as possible (sometimes I even throw a line in there that says, "I'm sure you're super busy..."). The shorter your email, the more likely you are to get a response. There have been times when people have cold emailed me and practically sent a book, and my first thought is, "Oh, this is not something I can read and reply to in five minutes, so I'll come back to it later." My second thought is, "Later may never come because I have so many other things to do that are much higher on my priority list." So keeping your email short is key. But one thing I want to add here, is that you want your email to be *visually* short. When someone opens your email, if they see a big chunk of black text, they may decide not to read it, just by looking at it. If that same big chunk of black text was split up by a lot of Enters, separating paragraphs (and even breaking paragraphs down into two), they will see more white space, making it seem visually shorter to read. White space is your friend. It can make an email seem shorter than it is, therefore, quicker to read. So I like to hit "Enter" more than just a regular paragraph break. I might hit "Enter" after every two sentences. You be the judge and see what makes sense, but one way to test it is to send it to yourself. I would check it on the phone and the computer and see if it appears like a long email. You don't have to do this every time...once you get the hang of it, you'll be able to tell quickly, but do a test in the beginning to judge the visual length.

**Be Complimentary:** You want to call out something they did that you can compliment. If you don't know anything specific they've done, it's okay to leave this part out, but I promise you, when you include it, it will make a difference. People want to know that you're not blanket emailing a bunch of people the exact same thing. Your email should feel personal. Do some research. Figure out if you have anything in common (like maybe you're from the same hometown). I always think it's good if you can compliment their work in a way that shows you're an expert. Speak the language of your craft. Say something that only an expert would say. For example, if I were emailing another graphic designer, instead of saying, "I loved your graphics in that episode!" I might say, "Oh my gosh, I loved that typography on the poster you designed! Crazily enough, the type designer for that typeface actually went to the same art school as me!" That's something a non-designer wouldn't say. It gives you more credibility and raises your chances of getting a response.

**Be Specific:** The last B, is all about specificity, and that's in relation the questions you ask. In your very first email, you don't want to make a big ask that will take a lot of their time. So you may not ask for coffee or a meeting or a job opportunity. Instead, I would ask a simpler question that they can answer quickly. Like, "How is a designer hired on a TV show? Is it through a design firm?" A designer could answer those questions very quickly. Also, remember, one of the goals is to potentially get your next steps. So a question you want to avoid is, "Do you have any advice?" I know it's very tempting to ask this question but I can't even tell you how much I loathe it. It's a cop out question because it will rarely give you an answer specific enough to actually help you. For example, if you asked me, "I want to move to LA! Do you have any advice?" I could reply with, "Sure! Be persistent and don't give up." That advice is not actually helpful in terms of your next steps. What do you really want to know? Make sure to keep your questions specific—oh, and only ask a couple questions. Don't send a list. Try to keep it under three questions.

If you get a response where they give you some specific advice, go do what they said! Nothing makes people happier than knowing you took action on what they suggested. It also shows that you're a go-getter, and not someone who is just "wishing and hoping" for their dreams. It shows you take direction well. So go do what they suggested and then email them back letting them know. Thank them for the advice, tell them that you did what they said, and share your results. They will love this and it will definitely increase your chances of forming a legitimate relationship.

## TRACKING YOUR EMAILS

One thing to note, is that this is essentially a numbers game. It may take 100 cold emails before you build a helpful connection, or it may take 3. Don't give up when you get discouraged. My clients and I love using a tool to help us track our email efforts because it helps you stay positive when you know your emails are opened and your links are clicked. When I was submitting this book to agents, I saw that one of my proposals had been opened 24 times! Even though it led to a rejection, it still showed me that they seriously considered my book and I must have something worthy of 24 opens. That was really exciting and helped me move forward, even after getting rejected. The tool I like to use is called BananaTag, but there are so many others out there, you can use whichever one you like. The most important piece of data to track is opens—if your emails are not being opened again and again, that's a good sign you should try changing your subject line. And speaking of trying a new subject line: remember that everything is an experiment. Your subject lines, what you say in your emails, it's all an experiment. So don't get too attached to what you write. You can switch it up and try new things if you're not getting good feedback. There is no single formula for this. Just follow the B's and you should be good!

Keep in mind that human connection is everything. If you're applying for a job at a big company, like Disney, for example, you're likely sending your resume through a computer that will analyze it and look for keywords. Big companies receive hundreds of applications, so it makes sense that a computer would weed through them before they get to a human. But that also means that a human is not evaluating your application unless it makes it through the computerized round. This is another opportunity to send a cold email. Try to connect to a human. They might be able to pass your resume along or support you in some other way. Look for people who work at the company, or in the department you're applying to (LinkedIn can be a great tool for this). Having a human on your side will always be more beneficial than a computer (no offense, my dear sweet iMac).

## POTENTIAL CONNECTIONS ARE EVERYWHERE

Cold emailing is a great way to take a Hard Action. It's an opportunity to actively seek out relationships in your industry. But potential connections are all around you, so it doesn't have to be the only way. I've met a handful of people through fitness classes. In Los Angeles, some of the high end fitness classes draw celebrities and known actors, so it's a great place to meet them. But please be normal. Do not stalk. Do not be obnoxious and bother people. Be. Normal. Approach them like you would a new friend. Let it happen organically.

I used to take a spin class in my neighborhood several times a week. It was mostly a pilates studio that happened to offer spin, so the spin classes were very small. There were only eight bikes, so pretty darn intimate! After taking this class almost every day, I slowly got to know the other students. It was impossible not to, being such a small class size. And spin class was a great equalizer. No one was special, we were all just trying to get through the class. I connected with some known actors there who ended up hiring me to work on their projects. I never forced anything, I let it happen naturally. And over time, relationships formed. It's so important to remember the marathon of it all. Your new relationships may not help you right this second, but over time, it could turn into the best help you've ever received.

I will never stop cold emailing. Every level of my career, I have new needs for connections. I love reaching out to people, knowing that eventually I'll get a response. I'll also open myself up to warm introductions through friends and other contacts. I'll ask the Universe to help me out and see where I'm led, so I lean into those passive solutions, too. But cold emailing and cold messaging on social media has led to jobs, opportunities, and incredible relationships, so I'll never stop doing it. Your people are out there. Keep believing that people want to help you. I know you may get unhelpful responses, or you may hear stories that everyone only cares about themselves. But I promise you, your people are out there. They have to be, because you're meant for this.

# Fourteen

# WHAT PERSISTENCE ACTUALLY LOOKS LIKE

Remember how I told you I was a huge theater nerd in high school? You may be wondering why I didn't pursue it in college. If I grew up acting and singing, why didn't I become an actor? Why a graphic designer? The main reason was because I fell in love with graphic design as I started designing the flyers and newsletters for the Drama Club. It really became a calling. But there is a second reason. And I want to share it with you because it has become a profound moment in my life that inspired me to help others.

It was senior year. I don't know how high school was for you, but for me, everything revolved around extracurriculars. If you played sports, that was your world. If you played an instrument, that was your world. I was secretary of the Drama Club and President of the Chorus, so that was my world. Everything revolved around theater, rather than academics. I marked my high school years by what musicals we did and what parts I got. It was my life. I remember one day in History class, I hadn't completed the homework that was due. I spent the night before designing the large scale diorama-esque showcase in the lobby in front of the theater as we prepped to advertise the upcoming show. Like I said, it was my life. I was designing this showcase until 11pm and enjoyed every minute of it. But this meant I didn't have time for the History class homework. When I told my teacher that I didn't have it, he looked me in the eye and reprimanded me. I remember it like it was yesterday because it was the first time I didn't flinch when a teacher called me out—I felt confident in my decision to design that showcase and I didn't care that it was my priority. I knew it was right for me. Actually, looking back, I feel like this was the first glimpse of my entrepreneurial spirit...making confident decisions about how I was spending my time, regardless if it fit what I was "supposed" to do.

By senior year, I had been a part of every musical and play the school put on. I was up for the lead more than once, even as a freshman. I was cast as the understudy to the lead my sophomore year. During a summer show, I played Kim in *Bye Bye Birdie*. All of this was great, but in our little theater bubble, I was never part of the top performing group. I was always on the outer edge. This information led me to believe I just wasn't good enough to pursue this after high school. I was good enough to participate, but I wasn't a star. And the stars in our school were all applying to the top drama programs in the country.

As acceptance letters started flowing in for those students, I longingly watched, wishing it was me. I just kept telling myself that I wasn't good enough...I wasn't on their level...only the best students at every school get into a collegiate drama program, and I wasn't one of them. One day, I sat down with my theater teacher for a conversation. It was just the two of us in a classroom. We spoke about college, and I said to her: *The reason I'm not pursuing acting in college is because I know I'm not good enough.* The little girl inside of me was desperately looking for my teacher to believe in me. I wanted to hear, "You are good enough, Erica! If you want to pursue acting, you should!" But that didn't come. Instead, she just looked at me in silence. That silence validated what I knew all along: I wasn't good enough to pursue my dreams.

I really do believe that everything happened for a reason, and graphic design became my true passion. I have no interest in acting now, and I love the career I've built. But I wanted to share this story with you because there was something my 17-year-old self didn't know that could have changed my entire trajectory: **talent isn't the only thing you need to succeed at a big dream.** Talent is only one tiny piece. After breaking into one of the hardest industries in the world, and living my dreams for over a decade, I've learned that there are so many other qualities that are required to succeed. I also recognize that I have all of those other qualities. And I wish my teacher was able to see that potential in me (actually...I take full responsibility—I wish *I* was able to see that potential in myself).

Over the years, I've discovered that these qualities are also necessary:
- Ambition
- Perseverance
- Self-discipline
- Dedication
- Resilience: get knocked down 7 times, get up 8
- Strong desire
- Unwavering belief in what's possible
- Willingness to ask for what I want
- Willingness to take risks

- Flexibility: ability to adapt and experiment
- Creativity: ability to see solutions and ideas
- Visionary: ability to see things that others deem "impossible"
- A positive mindset

Success at a high level requires all of those things. Talent, alone, will not guarantee success. Of all the students from my drama class who pursued acting or music in college, I think only one is actually doing it for a living. ONE! Of all those kids who were more talented than me and worthy of applying to theater school, only one has succeeded. And I'm the only one working in Hollywood.

Talent is something that can grow. It's something you can practice and work on. Plus...have you ever watched a movie or television show and thought the acting was bad? Have you ever listened to a song on the radio and thought the singing was bad? Some people even succeed without talent! The other qualities carried them through. And while we're here, the law of attraction doesn't care if you're talented. All it cares about is that you are a vibrational match for the thing you want. But I'm getting ahead of myself, we'll save that for Chapter 18...

Anyway, this isn't an Erica Pity Party chapter, I promise. I wanted to share this with you because now that I know, I want you to know, too. For all of those times you were told you weren't good enough, or those moments where you came to that conclusion on your own, I want you to know that you can do this. Your talent is not the single determining factor of whether you're "good enough." Instead, go through that list of other qualities. How many do you have? Put a check mark next to each one. The more you have, the more proof you have that you'll succeed. Regardless of your talent. Wait, does this mean your talent doesn't count?! No, no, no. I think you should have talent. Because, integrity. Work on your craft. Get better every day. But I want you to understand (in fact, this whole book's purpose is…) that you can do this regardless of what anyone has said to you about your talent. When you are meant for a dream, it's your *calling*. No external doubts can take that away from you.

We have to talk about this after the previous chapter because when you start cold emailing 100 people and none of them respond, your talent will not be the thing that helps you keep going. It will be your perseverance. It will be your discipline. It will be your dedication to your dream. It will be your belief or your knowing that you're supposed to do this. If you were really talented but didn't possess any of those other qualities, your dream would be a hobby and not a successful career. See the difference? Talent only gets you so far.

So what does perseverance actually look like? It looks like you continuing to move forward **until you get your dream**. It's really that simple. For me, it's always been that simple because of the desire in my heart. I can't *not* keep going. The desire drives me and that fire never stops burning. This doesn't mean I don't get discouraged or knocked down. I do. Plenty. But I always get back up. I always keep going. That's perseverance.

If the dream inside your heart feels really big, like something unreachable and nearly impossible, it makes sense that you may decide to have a "Plan B." It makes sense that you might draw up a plan that says if you don't achieve this in the next five years, you're throwing in the towel and pursuing something easier. Screw perseverance! You're trying to be "realistic!" But here's the honest truth: the only way that makes sense is if you don't believe your success is inevitable. Backup plans are created as insurance based on the belief that there is a possibility that this won't work out. I don't live in that world. That has never been my possibility, so I've never had a backup plan. When you're meant for this, there is no Plan B. There is only Plan A.

High Achievers do not put energy into a backup plan. I don't have time to entertain the idea, "What if this doesn't work?" That's such a waste of my energy! I only have space for strong belief. I only have space for knowing. I only have space for Plan A. Because it's not actually a plan. It's a *destiny*. And destiny doesn't need an alternative.

As you send cold emails or move through your strategy, you're going to experience rejection. You're going to experience delays. You're going to feel discouraged. You're going to feel impatient. Just because you're meant for this, doesn't mean the road will be without obstacles. As cheesy as it sounds, that's kind of the point. The journey to the dream is going to teach you so much more than the destination of the dream. And those lessons will contribute to the gifts you share with the world. Celebrate the obstacles—we've already established they are literally what success stories are made of. You're building your story now. Don't let it end prematurely. Don't stop before you've reached the pot of gold. Persevere.

Whenever my clients are in the midst of cold emailing or have an idea for an ask they want to make to one of their connections, there is almost always fear of "being annoying." I think this is particularly present with women. We tend to be more hesitant to ask for things than men. We think about how our question will be perceived and how we will come across. Will we piss them off? Will we bother them? Will they never want to hear from us again? These questions water down our ability to persevere. Because we're kind of hanging in there, but we're not really asking for anything. So we may still be in the game but we're not actually playing.

These fears are often much bigger in our head than they are in actuality. In fact, there is usually no reality attached to them at all. As long as you're a normal human being, you're not going to piss someone off by asking for what you want. If you do, then they're not your person. Most of us are capable of reading the room. You can gauge when the time is right, or how to phrase things. But when that fear takes over, your concern for the other person's potential reaction becomes more important than your dreams. It's great to be empathetic and care about other people (and, um, we could really use more of that from people in this country...) but as they say on an airplane: you have to put your oxygen mask on first. Your heart should be your priority over a stranger's potential reaction.

There have been times where I see people go too far. Once I connected an acquaintance to a friend of mine who offered to give them advice, but shortly after, that friend told me to have my acquaintance back off. They were emailing my friend all the time and crossing the line into obsessive territory. I also see actors do this with their email newsletters: actors get an email system like Mailchimp, add a bunch of casting directors to their list, and then send a mass email newsletter to them once a month. This is actually illegal. You can't add someone's email address to a list in an email marketing platform and send marketing emails to them without their permission. It's also very impersonal and if you learned anything from the previous chapter, it's to create a human connection. So it's always better to personalize each email. But these are the rare cases. Learn to read the room and you will be fine! Be respectful. Remember, you want to show that you're a great person to work with, so keep that in mind as you reach out to people. How you do one thing is how you do everything, so if you're overbearing in emails, that's a clear sign you'll be overbearing in work.

Now that I've scared you, we're off to a great start! Just kidding. Please don't be scared to ask for what you want! Just do it with tact. If you don't get any response at all, you can try following up in 3-5 days. If you do get a response, you can follow up once a month or once a quarter. Build that relationship over time. Persevere. Don't give up. If you do all of these things, and you keep going, it really is inevitable that you'll win.

There is a quote I've always loved that John Assaraf shares from one of his early mentors: "When you're interested, you'll do what's convenient. When you're committed, you do whatever it takes." It's so true, and one of the things that separates the people who succeed from the people who give up. You, you little High Achiever...you are committed. When you access your Star Power, you will do what it takes and always be prepared for what comes next. "Impossible" dreams are not for the interested. It's the interested people who call them "impossible." The committed people know that they will find a way. They persevere because they know, without a doubt, that the pot of gold is on the other side waiting for them.

The High Achiever builds their life around their dream instead of trying to fit their dream into their life. They make time for their dream. They have no backup plan. They keep going, no matter what. And it's not hard to do. It's not hard to persevere. Because it's a calling. It's bigger than a goal. It's bigger than a box to check. It's a dream that comes deep from the soul that demands to be heard. Persevere because you have to. Because you don't know any other way. Because you know this has to work out. Because any "Plan B" would be devastating. You're meant for this, so keep going until you get your "yes."

## PART 3

# The Star's Edge

*And, when you want something,*
*all the universe conspires in helping you get it.*
PAULO COELHO

# *Fifteen*

# BREAK THE ~~RULES~~ LIMITATIONS

personally know two Emmy winners, one Emmy nominee, and one Oscar nominee. One of my clients works for a pretty big A-list celebrity. I have friends who are regularly on TV. An acquaintance of mine was a lead on an incredibly popular show for all of its seven seasons. That blows my mind. When I started out in Hollywood, it felt like this big, out-of-reach industry. Now, it's so small. I'm a part of it. And despite the narrative that it's rare to succeed at a high level in Hollywood, I'm surrounded by people who have. I remember one time, a client was sharing a limiting belief that she's heard a lot: being successful in Hollywood is like winning the lottery. I asked her if she could name any people she actually knew who had won the lottery, and she couldn't name a single person. Then I asked her to name people she actually knew who were successful in Hollywood and she named at least ten. "See?!!" I replied. "You have proof that succeeding in

Hollywood is easier than winning the lottery."

I promise this isn't me about to name drop. I'm not *that* Hollywood. (If you heard me ask for a glass of "water", you'd know I'm really still so Philly. It's wooder.) In fact, I'm here to do the opposite: instead of evasively talking about my famous friends, I want to share everything I've learned from them. Because over the years, as I've watched their dreams come true, it's been very clear that they do things differently.

Remember those two pools we talked about in Chapter 1? The "Most People" pool and the "High Achievers" pool? There is a very specific reason why these famous friends of mine land in the second pool. Actually, there are three specific reasons, and I'm sharing them over the next three chapters. They do things that most people don't do. And that's why they're getting things that most people don't get, like winning Emmys.

My dream for you is that you don't just scratch the surface with your own dreams. I want you to live them in extraordinary ways. Yesterday in a coaching session with a client, I told her something that made her well up with tears. I said: *Your dream isn't just about you. When you're up on that stage, accepting your award for Best Director, all of the little girls in Asia will suddenly see what they've never seen before: that they're represented, that they matter, and that their dreams are possible. This dream of yours is bigger than you.* This client is originally from Thailand and never saw examples of her dream on screen. She wants to change that and show people back home what's truly possible. Her dream is bigger than her. And that's what happens when you feel like you're meant for something. That's why it's a calling.

To live an extraordinary life, you have to do things beyond the ordinary. And one of those things is to break the rules that keep you small. The rules (not laws, "rules") of your industry, of your dream, are statements that feel like they're set in stone because you hear them over and over again. They are rules that Most People abide by because they take them as the be-all-end-all of the industry. For example, in Hollywood, one of these "rules" is that you need a certain number of credits before you can move up to a leading role. It's a standard. It's part of the narrative that Most People buy into. But here's the most important thing you need to know about these rules: **There is always an exception. And that exception could be you.**

Any exception you find is proof that this rule is not the be-all-end-all solution. It's proof that solutions exist outside of those rules. Therefore, following those rules could keep you stuck where you are because you're allowing them to stop you from taking risks and doing things differently. With the Hollywood example, Alexis Bledel is an exception to that rule. She booked the role of Rory on *Gilmore Girls*, the leading titular role, without a single acting credit to her name. This is proof that the rule that states you need to have a certain number of credits before you can move up to a leading role, isn't always true. If it's not always true, why should you follow it?

The Emmy winners and award nominees that I know consistently break the rules throughout their careers. The rules are for ordinary people. They hold you back, they limit you. Extraordinary people don't waste time with them. They're here for extraordinary, so they show up powerfully. They skip levels. They ask for what they want. They don't wait to check boxes. Actors are often told to never submit to agents during pilot season. It's the busiest time of year for agents, as they pitch their clients to TV pilots, and they will "get mad" if you email them. The actors are told to only submit to agents certain months out of the year. Of course, I don't buy into that rule. So my clients submit to agents whenever they're ready: during pilot season, during episodic season, during a pandemic! And they always book agents when they do. Imagine if they followed the rule? Imagine if they waited to get representation until the rule says that it's okay? How many auditions would they have lost? How many money-making opportunities would they have lost? How much time would they have lost?

The key here is that **the rules limit you**. It's often that the rules will tell you not to do something. Or they will tell you to do it a certain way, and *only* that way. That's why I changed this title to *Break The Limitations*. The rules that stop you from taking an action or limit you, are the ones that hold you back the most. If you want extraordinary, those are the rules that must be broken.

Another actor client of mine said she finally felt ready for a Co-star role on a TV show. This means a role that has five lines or less. They usually don't have names; something like a waitress in a scene that says, "Can I take your order?" It's a small part that's usually the first type of television role an actor books. I said to my client, "How many years have you been studying acting?" She paused and started counting on her fingers. Pretty soon, she was out of fingers and replied, "At least ten. I've professionally studied acting for ten years."

I smiled. "OK, cool. Just so I'm clear: You've been studying your craft for TEN YEARS, and you're finally ready to say five lines on a TV show?" We both burst out laughing over the absurdity. She literally has enough education and practice under her belt that she would be considered an expert in any other industry. But the Hollywood "rules" had her doubting it and only feeling worthy of scraps. That's so f*$ked up! That's the power of rules. They play mind tricks and keep you playing small. Most people follow them. But you're not most people.

One thing I've noticed is that the longer people have been in Hollywood, the more rules they follow. They have more knowledge about how the industry works so they're aware of more rules. When people are just starting out, they're new and naive. The naiveté allows for imagination, creativity, and bold action. They don't have fears of doing it wrong because they don't know what the rules are yet. It's like being a child: you believe that anything is possible and you dream up the most imaginative ideas. When you're an adult, you have that real world experience to rain on your parade and limit the risks you take. You stop playing. You stop exploring. You stop questioning.

If you want exceptional results in your dream pursuit, you have to reconnect to your inner Visionary and see solutions that aren't part of the narrative. Netflix is an amazing example of this. For decades and decades, we all watched movies and TV shows the same way: on cable television whenever they aired. Let's call this the *rule*, shall we? The rule said this is how content is distributed. Then the internet came along and began to change things. We got platforms like YouTube and technology like cell phones that changed the way we created and shared content. Netflix noticed the trend and decided to disrupt the industry by breaking the rule. They didn't care that content had been distributed the same way forever. They didn't care that this was the "rule" in place. They saw the future and decided to be the visionary part of it. They changed distribution and they changed the business model. It obviously succeeded and not only does it dominate the market in content and awards, but the studios are now trying to catch up with their own streaming platforms thirteen years later. Thirteen freaking years! That's how far behind they are! All because Netflix had the balls to break the rules.

Think of what Netflix would have lost if they bought into the limitations of Hollywood. Think of the money, think of the content, think of the awards, think of the innovation! As a fan, think of what you would have lost. Think of the culture they created with Netflix and Chill and binge-watching. I feel like we're all pretty happy that Netflix went for it. It changed our lives, even in small ways. And believe it or not, your dream has the ability to do the same. That means your decision to break the rules could make or break the impact you have on someone's life. It becomes selfish of you not to go for it.

## BREAK THE RULES, NOT THE PROCESS

There is a lot of freedom in breaking the rules. If the rules are your shackles, breaking them is your freedom. You're no longer a prisoner and that can feel very freeing. But it's important to know what rules you're breaking, why you're breaking them, and what to do with that freedom. It should be calculated and intentional, not throwing the rule book out the window and having a party when your parents aren't home. You're not breaking the rules to stick it to the man, you're breaking free of limitations that are holding you back. This isn't meant to circumvent the process, it's meant to make the process work for you.

Before I became a designer full-time, I got to shadow another designer, and I also spent some time working as an assistant. Even though I felt ready to be a designer, I'm so glad I didn't skip the entire process. I quickly learned that there was a whole world I knew nothing about. I may have had a degree in Graphic Design, but I had never worked with a TV sign shop before. I didn't know what Sintra was or what widths it came in. I didn't know what legal clearances were or what it meant when my boss said, "These graphics play on Monday." The language of the art department was completely foregin to me and I had to learn it before I took a job that expected me to be fluent. I was able to break some of the rules and shorten the time I had to work as an entry level assistant, but I still lived through the process and learned which rules I could break and why.

Take inventory of the rules in your industry. What are you "supposed" to be doing? What are you "supposed" to avoid? There are two ways to easily spot them: 1) They use *absolutes*, words like "never," and "always" and 2) They stop you from taking an action. What rules have you been following so deeply that you've held yourself back? What have you been afraid to try? What assumptions have you made about avenues you've never tried? What limiting narratives have you taken on as your own?

The exceptional results don't lie in the ordinary rules. The exceptional results lie in the exception. That means you have to *be the exception*. You have to live in the energy in which you are the exception to the rule. You have to let go of the forced narrative and bet on yourself. The exceptional life you dream of is one broken rule away.

*Sixteen*

# OWN YOUR POWER

Your dream comes from the most powerful place: you. It's born from divine inspiration, one of the most powerful forces in the Universe. This calling becomes a burning desire, one that gives you ambition, perseverance, drive, and even compassion, in a way you've never felt before. It helps form the most powerful version of you there ever was. And yet, the moment it becomes an "impossible" feat you have to achieve, the power is immediately stripped away. It's your superpower and kryptonite all in one.

But the stripping of your power is really an illusion. It's a choice to give it away, and a choice you don't have to make. Instead of feeling at the mercy of others to make your dream come true, you can take your power back by realizing, as Abraham Hicks says, they are all just pawns in the law of attraction game. You get to control so much more than you think. You get to control your energy, your vibration, your beliefs, your strategy, your actions, your risks and asks, and the most important of them all—you get to create your reality. All of those things, combined with the belief in abundance and limitless opportunities, leads to a world where it doesn't matter if someone says yes or no to you—the dream is happening, no matter what.

I think one of my superpowers is reminding people how powerful they really are. That shift in energy can be all it takes to manifest exciting new opportunities. Because how you show up to the world is how the world will show up for you. Whatever you believe will be reflected back to you. If you feel powerless in your dream pursuit, you will have experiences that will confirm those feelings. And vice versa. P.S. Owning your power is so much more fun, so let's choose that, shall we?! Let me help you by busting the power myths that your subconscious is fighting for.

## GATEKEEPERS

Gatekeepers are like the bouncers of the club deciding who gets in. It feels like they have all the power, and artists are at the mercy of their decision. Actors are at the mercy of casting directors. Authors are at the mercy of publishers. Startups are at the mercy of investors. It feels like these gatekeepers are in charge of our fate and we have no control over what they say. Access to our dreams is in their hands. So how are we supposed to feel powerful in those moments? We hold none of the power in those decisions. *CLAP!* (That's me waking you up from the hypnotic spell you're under. Time for the powerful truth!)

**Powerful truth:** These gatekeepers do not determine your fate. Only you can do that. Pillar #7 says that your success is inevitable, which means your fate has already been decided. Any single gatekeeper or any single opportunity will not break your chances of succeeding. It's already been decided. Your success is a done deal. Who cares what this gatekeeper says? Your person is coming. Your opportunity is coming. Because it's inevitable. And if that's the case, what if these gatekeepers were, in fact, allies? What if they were friends? What if they were your support system, your cheer squad? What if the Universe always placed people on your path to help you? And what if that help didn't always come in the pretty package you want? A "No" could be just as much a gift as a "Yes." When Jack Canfield's book was turned down 144 times by publishers, what if that was all a gift because the publisher he was meant to work with happened to be the 145th? What if it's all working out perfectly?

We tend to put gatekeepers on pedestals because we think they hold the power. But YOU hold the power. Take them down from that pedestal, they are just people. They are pawns in your game. And this game is in the highest good of everyone. You know the value you bring. You know you were meant to do this, so it can't not work out. If this "gatekeeper" doesn't let you in, it says nothing about your potential. It says nothing about your future or your ability to succeed. It just wasn't a match. But I promise you, your people are out there. Keep going because they're looking for you, too.

## LUCK

I mean, I gave you a whole chapter on this, so I think we're good here. But I had to include it again because it contributes to the narrative that says you have no power in this dream pursuit. You have to get lucky and you have absolutely no power over that happening. It's out of your hands. *CLAP!* (Here we go again!)

**Powerful truth:** Now you know that's bullshit. Your success is not random. Your success is not accidental or up to chance. It's something you create. Because you have the power to do so.

## COMPETITION

It's hard to think we made it this far into the book without talking about this topic. When you walk into an office lobby full of competing participants, it's hard to nail that interview. Or when you think of the thousands of people who are fighting for the same success in the same arena as you, it feels impossible to feel confident. The concept of competition takes your power away. It says you have no control over who is chosen. It says the more competition you have, the lower your chances of winning. It says your chances are slim, so you better hope and pray. *CLAP!* (Yup.)

**Powerful truth:** Your success is inevitable, so the competition doesn't matter. You're going to win in the long run, no matter what. And that's true for everyone, so there is room for all of us. The only true competition is with yourself. Your happiness and joy is guaranteed, no matter who you're up against. And remember, success is a marathon. It's not the one-off competitions that matter, it's the sum of the whole. P.S. The feelings you think you'll get from an outcome are really the things to chase, not the specific outcome itself.

## COMPARISON

It's near impossible to make it through a dream pursuit without ever feeling jealous or comparing yourself to others. I catch myself doing it all the time. When you see someone further along than you, it can make you feel behind, hopeless, and unworthy. It completely strips you of your power. *CLAP* (This one is important!)

**Powerful truth:** You may have heard that comparison is the thief of joy, but it's also the thief of your power. As long as you compare yourself to others, you will always lose because there will always be someone ahead of you. But for every person ahead of you, they have their own countless disappointments and struggles. The timing or results of someone else's dream never takes your dream away from you. Your path is your own, and you've totally got this. Instead of comparing yourself to someone else, compare yourself to how far you've come.

## INAUTHENTICITY

This, this, this. The boxes you try to fit into will strip away all of your power. People will tell you to change yourself or do what "sells." You need to blend in, or you need to be like everyone else. You should emulate others who have succeeded before you. You need to replicate what they've done. Your industry only sees five solutions and you need to match one of them. If it's been proven to work, you need to be it, even if it's not who you truly are. Change your hair, change your weight, change your face. I was once told to speak more monotone to prospective clients and not show so much excitement. You need to *appear* a certain way. *CLAP!* (Oof, even I needed that one.)

**Powerful truth:** Listen to me, listen to me good—never, ever, ever, ever change who you are for your dreams. I mean, you can change your limiting beliefs into empowering ones. But you never have to be inauthentic. In fact, the more YOU you are, the more successful you will be. Because you have gifts unique to you and that's what we need. We need the you-iest version of you you've got! Take a look at some of the most famous artists today: Lizzo, The Rock, Taylor Swift...they are all their unique selves, not trying to be like anyone else. And that's what works. Want your power back? Be the most authentic you can be.

## DON'T GET YOUR HOPES UP

How many times have you heard this one? Or, better yet, how many times have you said this one? *I don't want to get my hopes up.* This one is the worst because when you feel momentum and things start looking good, you can't even enjoy it. You feel completely powerless because you have to protect yourself in case it doesn't work out. You are literally mentally preparing yourself for failure. And even if it starts to look good, you're waiting for the other shoe to drop. I mean, talk about angst! Can you ever be happy? Can you ever be hopeful? *CLAP!* (Oh hell yes, we're putting an end to this one right now.)

**Powerful truth:** It's okay to be excited. I know, what a revelation! It's good to feel hopeful about opportunities. If one doesn't work out, it is not a reason to feel down because abundance! So many more opportunities are coming your way. Instead of robbing yourself of hope, let yourself live in excited anticipation. That's actually the ideal emotion to feel when you're manifesting your desires. The energetic vibration of feeling hopeful in excited anticipation is much higher than the vibration of not getting your hopes up. That means getting your hopes up will actually help the opportunity manifest faster. Imagine that!

So instead of stopping yourself from feeling hopeful, stop yourself from getting attached. You don't need to get attached to any specific outcome. Let go of the specifics and trust that the Universe will bring you a solution that's in your ultimate, highest good. Now *that's* something to get hopeful about.

## TIME

Time is something we feel like we have no control over. And our instant gratification world makes us want everything now. "Erica, I'm so impatient!" I hear this 90 times a day. (Sometimes from myself...oops!)

Time holds the true power, not us. It's always held over us, like this thing we're always reaching for but never seem to catch. The timing of our dreams and when doors open is not up to us. How can you own your power when you feel a victim to time? *CLAP!* (I hope you're ready for this one.)

**Powerful truth:** What if you didn't care about the WHEN? Time only holds power over you because you care so much about it. But what if you didn't? What if it didn't matter? If your success was inevitable, then it really doesn't matter when it happens. We are impatient when we don't like our current circumstances and we think the dream will solve all our problems. We feel powerless to time when we're focused on everything we don't have. When lack is taking up the most space in our mind, we become very aware of time. This is an easy fix: slide into gratitude.

My Australian client and I have a running joke about time. Whenever we would schedule her calls, they would be 3pm on Wednesday in Los Angeles, and 9am Thursday in Sydney. Not only was it a different time of day for each of us, but a completely different day! A freaking day! Do you know how crazy that is? We were meeting together at the same time, but it was different times. This just proves that the way we see time is really just a label. During this coaching session, I'm labeling this hour as 3pm on Wednesday, and Anna is labeling it as 9am on Thursday. We define time in labels, when in reality, it's just the here and now. The Universe doesn't understand time the way we label it. Your dreams will happen in the perfect time, but not in a time specific to what you've labeled. Time is a concept, and when you let go of the labels, and trust in your success, you don't have to feel victim to it. Take that power back, you don't need to know when!

As you can see, the lack of power is just a myth. You can feel powerful at any point during this journey. And when you're able to own your power, you're going to create the reality you wish to see. You are in control of so much. You don't need to give your power away. Reclaim it. I remember the first chapter in Jack Canfield's *The Success Principles* was about taking responsibility for everything in your life. It's a scary concept because, man oh man, is it easier to blame other people or circumstances for whatever we don't like. But it's a powerful concept, too. Because it gives us our power back. If we are fully responsible for our lives, then we have the power to change them. We have the power to make our dreams happen. We have the power to create the opportunities we desire. And no one can take that away from us.

# Seventeen

# YOUR NEXT LEVEL

The other day in a podcast interview, I was asked, "How will you know when you've made it?" I love this question because when everyone starts out on their dream journey, they know a very specific destination they want to hit that will qualify them as "making it," but that destination tends to change as you start moving. We think when we hit a certain goal, that's when we'll be able to say we've made it. But after a decade of this journey, I promise you, that bar is always moving.

When I started building my business, I thought I would have made it when I hit six figures annually. It was a great accomplishment, but shortly after hitting that milestone, it didn't feel impressive anymore. People around me were hitting six figures *monthly*, making my "made it" goal seem like a joke. And that's when I realized that so many of my goals were based on how my success would look to other people. I didn't measure my success by how well my clients were doing or how many lives I helped change, but by how much money I was making. I wanted to be able to tell people, "My business does six figures." Which, now, seems so crazy. Because it's way more impressive to see the list of shows my clients have booked than the money in my bank account. It's more meaningful to me to know that I helped someone believe in themselves again, or I helped someone out of depression. That may not be as flashy as money, but it's become a more honest measure of success for me.

In Chapter 1, I encouraged you to set goals that were not based on external validation. Joy should be the real goal. What would make you so happy? And not because you'd get to brag about it to friends on social media, but because it would be challenging and fun. What would light you up? What would be SO exciting that you'd jump out of bed on a Monday morning for? That answer is going to change over time because once you accomplish it, the excitement may fizzle and you'll feel ready for your next challenge. That's what this chapter is all about: your next level.

Growth is a good thing. Even though you may feel greedy for wanting more or wanting something different than what you have, it's totally normal to need that growth. Your next level isn't always about the next rung on your ladder, but the growth that you're longing for. I think, especially as artists, we want new projects, new challenges, opportunities to learn new things. And as humans, we love the feeling of accomplishment. So when one accomplishment has run its course, it's natural that you'd seek out a new one.

But knowing you want your next level isn't the same as actually getting it. In fact, I've seen many people long for their next level but never actually hit it. That's mostly because your next level is your comfort zone's worst nightmare. It's unknown. It requires you to do things you haven't done before. And you're so comfy here with your tried and true strategies. Your subconscious mind will work overtime to try to keep you safe (i.e. where you are), no matter how badly you want it. The higher level achievements will require you to quiet those excuses. It will require your desire to be louder. It will require risks and leaps all over again (you thought you were done with those, ugh!). But it's nothing you can't do. Let's be honest, you were born to do this. Go, go, go! *Does a cheer jump with pompoms*

Getting to your next level is quite simple. It comes down to three methods, all that have been proven time and time again. And the second one is what got my friend those Emmy nominations (and a win!), so let's just say these methods are pretty badass. But did you expect anything less at this point, honestly?! High Achievers do things differently, and jumping levels is no exception. Before I dive into these three methods, let's make sure you're really ready for that next level. Here are four signs you're ready for more:

1.  **You feel internally ready.** It's easy to wait for someone to tell you you're ready for more, but the truth is, you are the only one who can answer that question. You are the only one who really knows what you're ready for. Do you feel confident about your ability to kickass at the next level? Someone else could take an educated guess, but at the end of the day, this is about internal readiness. And only you know that answer.

2.  **You feel worthy of the next level.** This is all about your self-worth. You need to feel worthy of what's next. You need to believe you deserve it. So many times, we compare ourselves from where we are

now to where we want to be, and then we feel like crap. Like when I saw other business owners making six figures a month. I wasn't there, and when I compared myself to that level, I felt unworthy. Instead of focusing on that gap, take a look back at how far you've come. See the levels you've already accomplished. Pat yourself on the back for a job well done. I mean, look how amazing you are! That's a great way to get out of lack and rebuild your self-worth.

3. **You mentally feel like you're already there.** This may sound kinda weird, but it's something I've noticed over the past two years in my own life. Once I said to my friend, "It's so weird. I feel like I'm mentally already there, but my bank account hasn't caught up yet." Have you ever felt that? Where you know you're ready but for some reason the physical stuff hasn't appeared yet? That's totally normal (and how manifestation works, anyway, so you're on the right track!). It's a good sign that you're ready for that next level.

4. **Your current level used to be exciting but now it feels a little boring.** Every new level will feel exciting in the beginning. But over time, it won't be new anymore and that excitement will fade. You'll miss being challenged. You won't look forward to these opportunities like you used to. This is a clear sign you're ready for what's next.

Before you make the jump, check in with yourself and see if you're really ready. When you are, prepare yourself. It's important to keep this in mind as you move forward: Reconnect to your Star Power. As I mentioned earlier, your subconscious is going to fight you on this so hard because it's outside your comfort zone. But you're meant for this, so you've totally got this. Push past the fear, embrace your affirmations, and take action. The three methods I'm going to share with you are in this section, *The Star's Edge*, for a reason. Most People are too afraid to implement these strategies. It's only for the High Achievers. This is the power behind the truly exceptional results and outcomes you desire. This will give you the edge. You ready? Let's do this.

## LEVEL UP METHOD #1: GRADUATE YOURSELF

This, this, this. Stop waiting for your industry to graduate you. Stop waiting for someone to tell you're ready for the next level. You need to actively seek it out yourself. This first method is all about deciding that you're ready and moving forward, regardless of whether another person has granted you the permission. When Reese Witherspoon decided she wanted to produce projects, particularly female-led books that turn into movies, TV shows, and limited series, the studios wouldn't take her seriously. They told her "No." I mean, that's Reese Freaking Witherspoon. An A-list star who has worked in the business for over two decades. So what did she do? She graduated herself. She started her own company and bet on herself. Reese wasn't going to wait for the industry to grant her permission, she was making that decision for herself. Reese's projects went on to be widely acclaimed and win countless awards. It wasn't until she had three successful projects: *Gone Girl*, *Wild*, and *Big Little Lies*, that the studios finally wanted to be in business with her. Isn't that crazy? Can you imagine if she waited for someone else to graduate her? If she waited for someone to give her permission? Hell. No. That's not how High Achievers play this game.

Graduating yourself takes courage because you're often going against the grain. You're doing things differently, and not how you're "supposed" to. When I chose to bump myself up to Graphic Designer and not take the middle-level job of Art Coordinator, I didn't care how others did it. I didn't care that most people take the longer path. I knew I was ready, so I claimed it. I didn't wait for it to come to me.

Decide that you're ready. Actively seek out your next level. Make the ask, prepare your portfolio, show proof that you can do this. Find people who will support you and let go of how it's usually done. You don't need anyone's permission but your own.

## LEVEL UP METHOD #2: BURN THE SHIPS

Are you paying attention? This is the one that led to all those Emmys.

A long time ago, back in 1519, Captain Cortés took his men into battle. They had to cross a large body of water, so the men got into their ships and sailed across the sea. When they arrived at the battle location, Captain Cortés said, "Men, we've arrived! Now I want you to burn the ships!" It sounds crazy pants, but he didn't want the men to get scared and have an easy way out. If they were afraid during battle, they could easily hop in their boat and sail back home. Cortes didn't want that option. He essentially wanted them to win or die. Without the safety net of the ships, the men had no choice but to succeed. (The crazy pants part wasn't totally off—I've read that this story isn't entirely true, but it has still been used in business for decades because of the great lesson, so let me use it!)

Burning the ships may be the scariest method, but also the most effective. It's about letting go of your safety net and forcing yourself to move up. This often involves turning down jobs or opportunities that are not in line with your next level. They may have served you well at your current level, but they're keeping you safe and holding you back from the next one.

Take Rachel Green, for example. (Yes, another *Friends* reference, I hope you're ready). Rachel worked in the coffee house as a waitress, but she really dreamed of working in fashion. Chandler and Joey confront her about it and here's how the conversation goes down:

**Joey:** Rach, wasn't this supposed to be a temporary thing? I thought you wanted to do fashion stuff?

**Rachel:** Well yeah, I'm still pursuing that.

**Chandler:** How, exactly are you pursuing that? You know, like, other than sending out resumes, what, two years ago?

**Rachel:** Well I'm also sending out good thoughts.

**Joey:** If you ask me, as long as you've got this job, you've got nothing pushing you to get another one. You need the fear!

**Rachel:** The fear?

**Chandler:** He's right. **If you quit this job, you then have motivation to go after a job you really want.**[5]

And that's burning the ships. It's letting go of the thing that's keeping you safe where you are, to help motivate you to go after your next level. (A disclaimer: you don't have to quit your day job like Rachel. Day jobs are good and help you pay for things like rent and food. But what other ways could you burn the ships?)

One example that pops up a lot in Hollywood is going from non-union projects to union projects. Nonunion projects are usually low budget like student films and short films, and some commercials. All of the films and TV shows you love are union projects, meaning everyone who works on them has to be in a union. Many people, actors especially, get scared to make the jump. If they join the union, that means they aren't allowed to do nonunion projects anymore. And those nonunion projects seem easier to get. So they're often told to stay nonunion as long as possible. But that's the "Most People" advice. When you're told to stay nonunion as long as possible, what they're really saying is, "Stay where you are as long as possible." It keeps you safe and comfortable. People are afraid to take the leap because they think the union projects will be so much harder to get so they don't want to give up these "easier" opportunities. But these "easier" opportunities are not at the level they dream of being. Most actors don't aspire to work on low budget films that may never be seen by large audiences. They aspire to work on studio and network projects that millions of people watch. And those projects require actors to be in the union. Instead of making a decision based on where they want to go, they are making a decision based on their fear. What if those old opportunities dry up? (Isn't that the point…?) What if the new, higher level projects never come? (Well, they won't with that attitude.) Joining the union and turning down nonunion projects is the equivalent of burning the ships. It's Rachel quitting her coffee house job. It forces you to get resourceful and make that next level happen. When you say "no" to old opportunities, you make room for the new ones.

My friend Kabir had a pretty successful career in reality television as an editor. He worked for prominent networks and worked consistently, which is a dream in this industry. One day, he was walking through the studio lot with his boss and had to pause because a scripted show was filming. Scripted TV was his dream and something he wanted to work towards. He turned to his boss and said, "Wow, so cool! When do you think we'll get projects like that?" His boss' reply changed everything for him. He said, "Oh, I don't want to do scripted. I actually love working in reality." That's when Kabir realized that if he kept doing what he was doing, he would never graduate to that next level he had been dreaming of. So a few months later, he quit the reality job and worked on getting a scripted show. He finally landed one, and was later nominated for three Emmys on that show and won once! Burning. The. Ships.

You can also do this with money. When I started working more consistently, I stopped taking jobs that were lower tier projects because it meant a decrease in pay by $15 an hour. That's a considerable difference and I didn't want to do that anymore. So any of those jobs that came my way, I politely declined. I know burning the ships can be scary. But think about it this way: you're raising your standards and no longer accepting anything that doesn't meet those standards. It's only natural that you'll begin to receive those standards. Stop making decisions based on fear. Start making them based on the next level you desire.

## LEVEL UP METHOD #3: NEW LEVEL, NEW STEPS

I'm sure this isn't the first time you're hearing this, but what got you here, won't get you there. Meaning, whatever strategies and tactics you've employed to get you where you currently are, most likely won't be the same strategies and tactics that will get you to the next level. It's not that your past steps were bad. They were awesome! They got you here! But your next level may require some different moves.

One of my clients, Jenny, is a Music Supervisor. She has done well and worked on many TV shows as part of a team. But she was feeling ready for her next level and wanted to take on more creative responsibility. So she decided to pursue this next level in a completely different way than what she had been doing: she started her own company. In the past, Jenny would move from show to show with her team, but never really getting the opportunity to move up. So she decided to break free of the team and go off on her own. People warned her not to do this. The Negative Nancies came out to share their "Most People" advice and told Jenny that shows would never hire a company. Well, I'm sure you know how this one ends because that's not how we do things at Hollywood Success Coach. Jenny started her company anyway, and in the first year alone, booked over a dozen network projects. Take *that*, naysayers! Jenny did a fantastic job utilizing this third method. She tried something new, regardless of how terrifying it was.

As I grow my business, I'll eventually have to hire employees. Because there is only so much I can do all by myself. So my next level will require new steps: hiring. Whatever got me to this point has obviously been great, but it's not going to get me to the next level. New level, new steps.

Take a look at your strategy. Is there anything you can do differently? Are there any new tactics you can try? It's so easy to say, "I'll just keep doing what I've been doing, and eventually it will get me there," especially when you believe luck and timing are the only reasons you haven't made the leap yet. But, as they say, that's the definition of insanity. Or, as Tony Robbins says, "If you do what you've always done, you'll get what you've always gotten." Your next level is literally about getting something different, so it's going to require you to do something different. Whether it's graduating yourself, burning the ships, taking on a new strategy, or a combination of all three, your next level needs you to take a leap. But it's nothing you can't handle.

Another thing to consider as you gain momentum: how can you leverage the success you've already created into more success? How can you leverage this level into your next level? How can you leverage one opportunity into another? You'll see celebrities starting their own fashion brands or writing a book after succeeding as a musician or actor. Some will explore a second medium after they succeed in the first one. This is leverage. They are leveraging their success from one area into another. Even at the micro level, you can do this with every opportunity you get. Think of your opportunities as a spider web—they branch out into other opportunities, as opposed to being a one-off. Can you make such a good impression that you're invited back? Can you get press to publicize what you've done, that leads to more opportunities? Can you create a social media campaign? Can you make a connection that hires you on another project? Leverage, baby! One success is not a one-hit-wonder, as long as you don't let it.

As the bar continues to move, and you continue to grow, you will easily have many "next levels." Come back to this chapter every time. The doubts will never stop coming and that imposter syndrome may creep up, but they will get easier to quiet. You'll become better at this process and pretty soon you'll be burning ships without even realizing it. It will be a no brainer thing you do. Keep climbing. Keep pursuing. Keep growing. The world needs your gifts at every level.

*Eighteen*

# EXPECT MIRACLES

wanted to start this chapter with a powerful example of how I've experienced miracles in my dream pursuit. As I sat down at the computer to write, I decided to search the internet for "Gabby Bernstein miracle" because it was through Gabby's work that I began to understand the concept of miracles. I thought it would spark an idea, and what I found was so much better: a miracle.

On Oprah's website, there was an excerpt of Gabby's book, *May Cause Miracles*. I've actually never read that book, but the first two paragraphs brought me to tears. It said:

*Winter 2009 was a turning point in my career. I was in the process of trying to get a publishing deal for my first book,* Add More~ing to Your Life: A Hip Guide to Happiness. *At this time the recession had us in a headlock.*

*Fear and uncertainty were at an all-time high, news anchors reported on the ever-growing unemployment rates, and nearly every industry was negatively affected.*

*I remember sitting in my mother's kitchen telling my stepfather about my book concept. He tried his best to be as supportive as possible, but his fear of the recession was very strong. He responded, "This is a great concept, Gab, but don't forget that right now is a terrible time for the economy. It will be hard to sell a book." My response was confident and almost involuntary—words flooded out of my mouth. "Thank you for sharing," I said. "But I don't think that way because I believe in miracles." I felt empowered by these words and filled with faith regardless of the outside world's resistance. In that moment I witnessed my commitment to letting go of fear and recalibrated my faith in miracles.[6]*

At the time of writing this, I'm in the process of trying to get this book published, in the middle of the COVID-19 pandemic. Fear and uncertainty are at an all time high, news anchors are reporting on the ever-growing unemployment rates, and nearly every industry is negatively affected. I couldn't believe what I was reading. It was as if the Universe delivered me a little present, all wrapped up with a pretty bow. It was an uncanny message that I couldn't *not* feel connected to. A moment of faith and inspiration placed on my path, telling me to keep going. This is a miracle.

Over the past twelve years, my faith in my dreams has been tested many times. I've experienced doubt, depression, and days where I want to give up. My will to continue always came from the desire—because I felt I was meant to do this. Even in my darkest moments, I would still believe. My belief actually astounds me sometimes—it's pretty incredible to see how determined I am, even when I'm on the floor in tears. This journey can be exhausting. And as much as you need to be strategic and take risks and do those hard actions every day, there are going to be moments where you need to rely on something intangible: faith.

I've always been a hopeless romantic, but not just about love. I'm a hopeless romantic about everything, particularly dreams. (Have you not noticed?) I believe in movie-level magic. I believe in signs from the Universe. I believe in miracles. And I think that spiritual connection is what helps me make it through. The romanticization I create of the dream journey is what led me to write this book. Because I really do believe in some divine force that helps us make even our most "impossible" dreams come true. That's why I'm not jaded or cynical, even after all these years in Hollywood. I believe in the romance of it all, forever, and ever.

After my first TV show was cancelled, it took me almost nine months to find another job—and I mean *any* job. The economy had crashed and I couldn't even get a waitressing job. It was the hardest nine months of my life. During that time, I had my first experience with situational depression. I never left the apartment. I hid in my room most of those nine months. Since I didn't have an income, I couldn't spend money. I was living off tiny savings I had grown and it was the tightest budget of my life. Fortunately, I never lost my home. But I felt like I had lost so many other things. I remember one day I went to Rite Aid to get the one or two items I could afford, and as I stood in line, I felt so envious of the people who had more than two items in their basket. Tears welled up in my eyes as I watched people freely pay for their things. The anxiety I felt when it was my turn has never really left me all these years later. I still feel that memorized fear when the cashier rings me up at Target or the grocery store. Even with more money in my bank account, the anxiety lives on.

It was a really hard time, but as I look back, I can easily spot the miracles that appeared to help me survive. They were small to some, but epic to me at the time. On Saturdays, I would go to a synagogue I liked for Shabbat services. It was partly because I felt less alone, and it was nice to feel like I was praying, but it was mostly because they offered a free lunch afterwards. This was my chance to get free food. It may sound silly, but that was a miracle I was led to.

One of my roommates at the time had the entire *Friends* series on DVD (this was way before Netflix had it streaming). She let me borrow it, and I would lock myself in my room all day, watching season after season. The brightness and the comedy helped me get through the day. That's why I'm obsessed with the show. This was a miracle.

I started writing music as a form of therapy. A friend let me have his old keyboard for free (miracle), and I would write sappy sad songs about my life. It's cliché, but I know it helped me process my feelings in a healthy way. I even performed them at open mic nights. I thought I was Sara Bareilles or something. My songs were not that great, but the hope the experience gave me was. Miracle.

One day, I found myself at my rock bottom, crying to my Dad's cousin who lived in Los Angeles. We barely knew each other before I moved to LA, as I had only met her one time at a funeral, but she quickly became my entire local support system. As tears streamed down my face, she told me a story that helped me understand it's okay to ask for help. That's when I started opening up to friends (after ghosting their calls and texts for months), and one of those friends helped me book my next job on the most popular show in town: *Glee*.

I know the world "miracle" has been defined many times by many different outlets, and usually makes us believe that it's a grand gesture from God that is so mind blowing, it only happens in the movies (or the Bible). But through the words of Gabby Bernstein, and a cheesy movie or two, I've come to decide that miracles are much more accessible, and they happen every day. Gabby Bernstein says that if you're not experiencing miracles, something is wrong. It means you're living from fear, instead of from love. The absences of miracles is the absence of love. Miracles, for me, are an act of grace. They can be small. They can be big. And they really do occur every day. They are so common and natural, that you should come to *expect* them.

So much of going for these big dreams you feel meant for, is about trust. We have to trust that it's coming. We have to trust that we're doing it right. We have to trust that we're being led to it. It's the ultimate energetic surrender. We set our intentions, we take the actions, and we trust. Miracles are placed on our path to help us keep that faith. Sometimes they pop out of nowhere. Sometimes they're small enough to fly under our radar but grand enough to help us turn a bad day into a good one. It's the coincidences. It's the oh-my-gosh-I-can't-believe-that-happened moments. It's the tiny gifts that help our journey feel easier. It's the proof we want to help us feel like something bigger is helping us. It's how we know we're meant for this.

Miracles range from the mundane to the mammoth. It can be an opportunity opening up because someone had to drop out. It can be a post on Facebook that you just happen to see about an amazing connection. It can be a free cup of coffee. It can be a friend who shows you support when you need it. It can be a door opening that you're coincidentally prepared for. It can be an answer to your prayers. Miracles occur all the time, especially when you know to look for them.

We've all been taught to look for potholes when it comes to pursuing a dream. We're taught to look for egos and crappy odds. We're taught to look for a backup plan. All our lives, we've been trained to see our dream pursuit as glass-half-empty. And as you recall, we get what we believe. We get what we're seeking. So if we're seeking half-assed opportunities that are sure to ruin our chances, then that's exactly what we'll find. I'm writing this book because I want to change that very narrative. Instead of expecting the worst, I want you to expect miracles.

What would your life look like if you expected success? If you expected things to work out? If you expected miracles? I know the other discouraging narrative is so ingrained in you that your first reaction may be, "If I expected success, I would surely be disappointed." Now is the time to change those old beliefs. Now is the time to let go of that pattern. Start small. I dare you to expect one teensy tiny miracle over the next five days. Look for it. Expect it. And report back. As Abraham Hicks always says, it's just as easy to manifest a castle as it is a button. So if you can find one teensy tiny miracle this week, you can find a grandiose one next month. It's all working in your favor when you know to look for it.

In his book *Playing The Matrix*, Mike Dooley has a great metaphor that I want to share with you. Imagine you're sitting in your car in the garage. You plug in your destination to the GPS, but no directions are appearing yet. The GPS keeps telling you to get on an actual road, and then the directions will begin. You have to put your foot on the gas, reverse out of the garage, and start driving in order for the directions to kick in. Once you do, that's when the GPS will tell you turn right or go straight for three miles. It's the same thing with the universal guidance you'll receive on this dream journey. You have to start taking action in order to activate the directions. Once you put your foot on the gas and make a move, that's when you'll get those nudges to take this class or email that person. And the miracles you receive along the way will be the Universe's way of letting you know you're on the right track.

I was never a super spiritual person until I started pursuing my dreams. The spiritual practice became a lifeline. Even when you're armed with all the tools in this book, you still have moments where you need a hug, or someone to tell you to keep going. That's what my spiritual practice has done for me. And when I say "spiritual practice" I'm exaggerating a bit because it's not that defined and it's not that consistent. Some days it looks like meditating, some days it looks like listening to motivational speeches, some days it's reading a book, some days it's repeating affirmations, and some days it's surrendering my fears in front of the ocean. Some days it's just trying really hard to practice patience. But I think *all* days, I'm believing in the potential that is available to me. *All* days, I'm trusting and surrendering. *All* days, I'm betting on myself and knowing the Universe is betting on me, too.

I'm not here to tell you to become more spiritual. It's up to you to find whatever helps you through the uncertainty. But I do encourage you to expect miracles. I do want you to expect things to happen for you. Believe that everything is working out for you, even when it feels like it isn't. I'm rooting for you. The Universe is rooting for you. You should root for you, too.

# *Nineteen*

# KINDNESS, INCLUSIVITY, & SPREADING THE LIGHT

"This is the layout for the wedding," the Set Decorator explained. THE WEDDING??! WHOSE WEDDING?? I almost peed my pants with excitement. (Except I totally played it cool and showed my stark poker face.) These are the champagne problems of working on a show you're a fan of. The Decorator looked at me as I quietly sat listening, and said, "Can you go make two copies of this? Thanks." I didn't hesitate for a second, even though I didn't actually work there. An hour earlier, I was walking around the Paramount Studios lot and peeked into the Prop Master's office on the set of *This Is Us*. We had worked together on a previous show, and I was at Paramount Studios often, so I frequently popped in to say hello. This time, he was called into a meeting with the Set Decorator, and instead of leaving like a normal person, I ended up following him and joining in on the three person meeting. So *of course*, I appeared to be a PA, and not just a friend stopping by for a visit. Especially on this super secret meeting about the season finale of one of the most popular shows on television. I don't fault her for asking me to make photocopies of a set drawing. The crazy ironic thing was that the art department for *This Is Us* was in the same bungalow that I was in for *Glee* ten years ago....when I was a PA. So I was practically making photocopies on the same copier, living out a very familiar task. Only this time, I was suddenly privy to top secret information about a wedding! On *Glee*, it was usually top secret information about a musical number.

How did I end up here? How did I visit Paramount Studios in the first place, when I wasn't working on a show? How did I end up hanging out on the set of *This Is Us* for so long? It all comes down to one word: kindness. Please don't barf all over that cliché. I am so serious! I remember a few years ago, when I went to my high school friend's wedding, people were asking me all about Hollywood. I was curious as to what I seemed like from the outside, so I asked one of them, "Do I seem all 'Hollywood' to you?" I was relieved that they replied with, "Not at all! You're the same old Erica." I've always made kindness a priority, and not because it's a strategy, but because it's who I genuinely am. I love befriending people I work with, it makes the work day so much more fun. I am nice to everyone, whether you're the janitor who cleans the room at the end of the day, or the Executive Producer. Of course, that kindness is not always reciprocated, but when it is, it always leads to great opportunities, like visiting the studio lot and hanging out at *This Is Us*. These people have become genuine friends because I've always been kind.

The reason I wanted to tell you this, is because I know this book will help people achieve their dreams at high levels. I know one day you'll be the head of the studio, or the CEO of a company. And I feel I have a duty to encourage you to be kind, include and accept everyone, and help spread the light so this work can impact people in a ripple effect. Whenever I have actors in my coaching program, I always train them to be kind leaders when they become Number One on the call sheet. "Number One on the call sheet" is what we call the lead of the show, as they are listed first in the order of the cast. Number One on the call sheet has the opportunity to set the tone of the show. They have the chance to create a fun, loving, inclusive atmosphere where everyone feels appreciated and enjoys coming to work. Their attitude can affect the entire feel of the show, from the actors down to the production assistants. People's livelihoods are in their hands, so I want my clients to create a positive atmosphere for everyone they work with. I want them to be responsible for a crew member saying, "I love working here!" That joy doesn't end with that crew member. That crew member will take it home to their spouse and their children. They will be more joyful and present at home. They won't be full of anxiety about Monday. And this will domino throughout their community. When you are in a leadership position, you have the power to create joy. And that isn't a responsibility to take lightly.

It's also an opportunity to be inclusive. My hope is that this book helps create a new generation of powerful leaders who create the change we want to see. We need to bring all different kinds of voices to the table. We need representation that actually represents what we see in the world around us. As you collaborate with people and advance in your dream pursuit, be conscious of who you're inviting to join you. Diverse people will bring diverse ideas and you can't put a price tag on that. The stories you'll create when you listen to and include people from all races, all genders, all sexual preferences and all socioeconomic backgrounds, will expand the light in ways you can't even imagine. We have the power to inspire others. We have the power to empower others. We have the power to create a new tomorrow, one that is full of empathy and understanding. And those stories and experiences will be so much richer than through our own limited lens.

High Achievers have a responsibility to pass on the wealth. Wealth of knowledge, wealth of confidence, wealth of creativity, wealth of power. I can't say it enough: when you're meant for something, it's going to be about so much more than just you. There are so many lives you're going to impact. You are going to make a difference for so many people. Don't take that lightly. Have gratitude for them and be conscious of what you're putting out into the world. I was fortunate enough to work on some shows that literally saved lives. People would write into *Glee*, and share how it helped them come out to their parents. On *Chasing Life*, people finally felt less alone going through their cancer treatments. Even though my role in those shows was small, it still makes me feel so good to know I was part of it.

The more kindness you exhibit, and the more accepting you are, the further you will go in this dream pursuit. Remember, this journey is so dependent upon relationships. And you'll make strong ones when you make people feel good. But don't do it because it's a strategy to help you get ahead. Do it because it's the right thing to do. Do it because it could make a difference in someone's life. As Maya Angelou says, *People will forget what you said, people will forget what you did, but people will never forget how you made them feel.* When you make people feel good, they'll want to support you. They'll want to help you and be part of whatever you're creating. Your belief will become contagious. If we can get more people believing in their dreams, and successfully going after them, we'll have more inventions, more service, more contributions, more leaders, and at the very least, more joy. It's up to us to spread that light. You with me? #TeamKindnessAndJoy

# Twenty

# ALWAYS WINNABLE

Have you ever played Solitaire on your phone? Does that show my age? I'm playing Solitaire, not Candy Crush, or whatever the kids are playing these days. I'm old school. Or maybe just old (Oy!). Whenever I play Solitaire on my phone and choose to play an "Easy" or "Medium" level game, little text comes up to tell me: *These games are always winnable.*

This means that if I play the game and get stuck, I can hit "replay" or I can undo a bunch of times. Either way, the game is always winnable, so if I'm not winning, all I need to do is try different moves. Since I know it's always winnable, I'll never give up until I win. Even if that means starting over 10 times, or asking for a hint. It would be embarrassing to quit a game that is literally winnable. The other day I was playing a game that I really struggled with. I restarted 5 times and still couldn't win. It was frustrating, but not in a hopeless way, because I knew it was winnable. It became a fun challenge. There was something exciting about trying to find a solution when I knew one definitely existed. It's different to play a game that isn't guaranteed winnable—to get stuck and not even know if a solution exists. The "Hard" level games are not always winnable. So if I get stuck on one of those games, I give up so much faster than I do on the always winnable games. I might replay it a few times, but eventually I'll just move on to a new game. With the always winnable games, I never move on until it's solved.

I truly believe your dream is just like those Solitaire games: always winnable. You may have to try some new moves or get a do over, but it is always winnable. If you feel meant for something, how can it not be? I don't believe the Universe is cruel and dangles our dreams in front of us to taunt us. We were given these dreams for a reason. Therefore, it has to be winnable.

Knowing it's always winnable is a game changer. Just like I would eventually give up on the "Hard" level games because there was no guaranteed win possible, when you don't believe your dream has a guaranteed win, it's easier to give up trying. You'd feel like you're working so hard with no guarantee and you don't want to wait any longer to see if the reward eventually comes. But what if you knew your dream was winnable? What if it was guaranteed? What would you do differently? How would you approach it? What would you do when you felt stuck? When your dream is always winnable, it brings back the joy. It becomes a puzzle to solve that challenges you and forces you to get creative, rather than a dead end.

After playing for a while, I came up with a new strategy (yes, I'm still talking about Solitaire, stay with me man!): instead of placing every card I could, I started prioritizing revealing the facedown cards. Uncovering all the cards was the key to winning, so I decided to focus on that. I noticed when I did, I always won, and usually faster than the other way. But oh-my-gosh this was hard to implement in the beginning! Every time I had a card that I could easily place down, it was so hard to have the willpower to skip it, if it didn't help uncover one of the facedown cards. So if a three of clubs was my next card, and there was a pretty red four of diamonds sitting there, waiting for a black three, I wouldn't place it there unless it helped uncover other cards. Putting that three on the four was so habitual...it's how I used to play. I had to fight the urge and wait until I uncovered more cards.

As you pursue your biggest dreams, you'll have to try new strategies. You'll have to leap outside your comfort zone, even though you desperately want to stay comfortable where you are. The old way of doing things will literally be a habit—a habit that you need to break. You'll have to fight the urge to do things how you used to do them. But the new ways will help you gain momentum and soon it will become easier to do all the uncomfortable things.

Trust your intuition and where it wants to lead you. Whenever clients tell me they're not sure what dream they want to pursue, it's always revealed that they *do* know what they want, they're just too afraid to admit it or say it out loud. Or if they're unsure of a decision and want help talking it out—they're usually just asking permission to make the choice they want to make. Our intuition has all the answers we seek. Start listening to it. Trust in your own voice. It will always lead you where you want to go.

If I could leave you with anything at the end of this book, it's that your dreams are always winnable. People will disagree. They will tear you down and discourage you from going for it. Tune those voices out and start listening to your own. Your inner being knows the truth. Every dream is possible. No matter who you are. No matter where you come from. No matter how "impossible" it seems. You are so much more powerful than you realize. The potential you have is guaranteed because you were given this dream. It's really that simple. And yes, I may be a hopeless romantic here, relying on the magic that movies have provided fictionally for years, but this is the world I love to live in. Life is so much fuller, so much more exciting, so much more hopeful. And it works. I'm living proof.

I'll leave you with this:
*You can do this*
*Believe in yourself*
*Your dreams are worth pursuing*
*To follow a dream is to follow joy…*
*Is to follow the light…*
*Is to follow love…*
*You don't need permission…*
*You don't need validation…*
*Just because it's hard*
*Just because the path is unknown*
*Doesn't mean you shouldn't do this…*
*You were given this dream for a reason*
*It comes from within*
*It comes from the divine*
*You are meant for this because you decide you are*
*No one can take this from you*
*You are the creator of your destiny*
*Believe you can, and you will*
*Keep going*

*There will be obstacles*
*But you can run through them*
*It's not just for you*
*It's for all of the people whose lives will be impacted*
*You have a gift*
*You must share it with the world*
*People's lives are going to be better because of what you bring to it*
*This isn't just about you*
*Get past your fears*
*You have to do this*
*There is a reason you were sent this dream*
*There is a reason you felt called to this*
*It's up to you to find out what that reason is*
*When we were children, it was so easy to dream*
*We believed we could do anything*
*The possibility that we couldn't, didn't even exist in our mind*
*We didn't know failure yet*
*Or at least the way we define failure as adults*
*Failure is simply something that didn't work*
*It doesn't mean you aren't loved*
*It doesn't mean you aren't accepted*
*It just means you are one step closer to everything working out*
*And it will*
*Because you are meant for this*

Every dream is possible. Your dream is always winnable. You are meant for this.

# NOTES

1. Dr. Joe Dispenza, *Breaking The Habit Of Being Yourself* (United States: Hay House, 2012).
2. Tony Robbins, "6 Basic Needs That Make Us Tick," December 4, 2014, https://www.entrepreneur.com/article/240441
3. Dr. Joe Dispenza, *Breaking The Habit Of Being Yourself* (United States: Hay House, 2012).
4. Chicken Soup For The Soul, "Facts and Figures," https://www.chickensoup.com/about/facts-and-figures
5. *Friends*. "The One Where Rachel Quits." Season 3, Episode 10. Directedy by Terry Hughes. Written by David Crane, Marta Kauffman, Michael Curtis, Greg Malins. NBC, December 12, 1996.
6. Gabrielle Bernstein, *May Cause Miracles* (United States: Harmony Books, 2013)

# Acknowledgements

Just like with any big dream, we don't get very far without the help and support of others. This entire book journey wouldn't be anything without some amazing people in my life. I feel like I'm about to write an Oscar speech, which is so ironic! But here we go:

First, I'd like to thank my parents! (This might go a little long, please don't play me off stage with that music.) My Mom and Dad have supported every "crazy" dream I've ever had. They are the first people I call for everything: when something exciting happens, when I'm crying and wondering why it hasn't happened yet, when I have a new idea. They support me through it all. They've even let me drag them to $15 million dollar open houses. What does that have to do with this book? Well, everything. Because this book is the culmination of everything I've learned over the past 12 years...a journey that wouldn't be as successful without their support. They are truly the best.

Next, is my cousin Meryl. She introduced me to the self-help world and I couldn't be more grateful. Who knew that giving me Jack Canfield's book all those years ago would lead to this?! Thank God Meryl lives in LA, because without her, I wouldn't have any family out here in California. Meryl has been one of my biggest advocates and the person I could turn to to get advice about every business endeavor. Her no-bullshit attitude was just what I needed to thrive in this path. Thank you, Meryl, for everything you've done for me, including reading everything I sent your way in the early stages of this book. I'm still working on that house for us. That gluten-free chef is coming!

There were a handful of early readers that gave me the confidence I needed to continue. Amanda Durocher, Kyle Higman, Amanda Kruger, and Malak Dabcha. THANK YOU. I was so nervous to put this out into the world and your feedback and support has helped me more than you know. Derek Doepker helped me come up with this title and held the space while I brainstormed a bunch of really bad options! Derek, you've always been a cheerleader of my work, and I am so grateful for that.

Carrie Stiers, the astrologer psychic I reach out to whenever I need to hear, "Everything's going to be okay, Erica!" You encouraged me to write the full book, even while still reaching out to publishers, and that advice made a huge difference for me. It's one thing to write an outline and a few chapters, but writing this full book helped me to remember the value I have to offer. That's priceless. Thank you for the nudge, Carrie.

I told you this was long...DON'T PLAY THE MUSIC!! I've got more...

Ginger Marie Corwin, you brought me to that Gabby event where my inspired wheels finally began to turn. This book was born there. I have no doubt you intuitively knew to invite me along.

Stephen Lovegrove, on the days I began doubting myself after many rejections, you built me back up. Your belief in this book helped me to keep going. I hope you know how much that means to me.

Aunt Lynda, you bought my t-shirt, you ask about every step of every project, and you've supported me just as much as my parents. I am so grateful for you. I hope you think my book is "not bad."

I also want to give a shout-out to every client in the HSC family. You guys inspire me. I feel so fortunate to get to coach you and it's because of you that I even have the content for this book. You're out there, doing the work, pursuing your dreams against all odds the world has thrown at you. I never see you as anything less than stars. I love you all so much and I thank you for allowing me to be part of your journey. This book is for you. I hope it inspires you to dream bigger, picks you up off the ground when you need a friend, and helps you continue to believe in yourself so much that your confidence becomes contagious. Let's spread the light and change the world.

Okay, now you can *cue music*.

# About the Author

Twelve years ago, Erica had a dream of working in Hollywood, but she didn't know a soul and had zero connections. Despite all this, Erica was able to break in and booked her first TV show just two weeks after moving to LA. Over the past decade, Erica has lived her dream, designing graphics for television and film. You can see her work on hit shows like *Glee*, *The Office*, *Superstore*, and most recently *Top Chef*. After fulfilling her own dream, Erica felt called to help other Hollywood creatives with their dreams, and started a coaching business. Since then, Erica has developed a reputation as Hollywood's Leading Success Coach, and between herself and her clients, they've booked work on over 60 television shows and films on every major network, including Netflix, Hulu, HBO, and more.

*For more resources, visit Erica's website at hollywoodsuccesscoach.com. You can also follow Erica on Instagram @hollywoodsuccesscoach and listen to her podcast, The Hollywood Success Podcast, on Apple Podcasts and Spotify.*

*Erica loves hearing your success stories, so don't hesitate to send them over! You can tag her on Instagram or email to hello@hollywoodsuccesscoach.com.*